NEGRO CULTURE IN WEST AFRICA

A SOCIAL STUDY OF THE NEGRO GROUP OF VAI-SPEAKING PEOPLE
WITH ITS OWN INVENTED ALPHABET AND WRITTEN LAN-
GUAGE SHOWN IN TWO CHARTS AND SIX ENGRAVINGS
OF VAI SCRIPT, TWENTY-SIX ILLUSTRATIONS OF
THEIR ARTS AND LIFE, FIFTY FOLKLORE STOR-
IES, ONE HUNDRED AND FOURTEEN PRO-
VERBS AND ONE MAP

By

GEORGE W. ELLIS, K.C., F.R.G.S.

ISBN: 978-1-63923-854-5

Printed: March 2023

Published and Distributed By:
Lushena Books
607 Country Club Drive, Unit E
Bensenville, IL 60106
www.lushenabks.com

ISBN: 978-1-63923-854-5

YOUNG VAI WOMAN

To my mother
AMANDA JANE ELLIS
whose thrift and industry rendered me indispensable aid and assistance in all my efforts for educational advancement, and whose unsullied life and Christian character remain to me a perpetual source of inspiration to lofty thought and noble achievement, this volume is gratefully and respectfully dedicated.

TABLE OF CONTENTS

TABLE OF CONTENTS

LIST OF ILLUSTRATIONS

INTRODUCTION

"Negro Culture in West Africa" needs no word of praise from my pen; it stands fairly upon its own merits. But its appearance justifies a brief introduction. However uncertain many of the teachings of ethnology in regard to Africa may be, we may quite sharply distinguish two masses among its dark peoples — the Bantu peoples in the south and the true Negroes further north. The division is based primarily upon language, but it is well borne out by physical type and by culture. The people to whom Mr. Ellis introduces us are representative true Negroes of West Africa. What he tells us regarding them will be true, for the most part, of all the populations lying to the south of the great desert and north of the Congo basin and stretching across the continent from the Atlantic to the Indian Ocean. The special population, which he has studied, is the Vai (or Vei), lying in the neighborhood of Cape Mount and occupying a considerable area stretching back into the hinterland.

They are by no means a decadent folk. They are vigorous, energetic, enterprising. Not only are they physically splendid, they are shrewd and acute in mind. They are Mohammedans, and that means that they are independent, even aggressive, in attitude. It is unnecessary for me to sketch their character and life; Mr. Ellis treats both in detail. But we may say that no people on the West Coast of Africa can better be taken as typical

and showing what the African can do, either when left
to himself or when affected by outside influences. It
was among the Vai that the only practical and actually-
used script for the writing of an African Negro language
has been produced. Mr. Ellis tells us of it and of its
inventor Doalu Búkere. The name of this Negro Cad-
mus deserves to be remembered, and from a people which
produces such a man, something is justly expected in
the present and in the future. So far as the present is
concerned, the Vai population includes a plenty of
shrewd, intelligent, industrious and useful men. It is
new to most of the readers of this book, that there are
Vai native Africans of pure blood, who possess libraries
of Arabic books touching upon a considerable range of
subjects. Among the Vai are men like Momolu Massaquoi, who are useful alike to their own people and to the
Americo-Liberians. His experiment of preparing text
books in Vai, printed in Doalu Búkere's script will be
watched with interest. From among the boys of his
people many may be stimulated by the study of books in
their own language and script to strive for high achievement. To the Vai the Honorable J. B. McCritty, present Mayor of the City of Monrovia, traces much of his
blood and unquestioned ability.

The Vai are chiefly a Liberian population. There are
many tribes of natives in the Republic, differing from
each other in language, in character, in life. They may
be rather readily divided into three groups. There are
(a) pagan people, in the interior, in large part hardly
affected by the outside world, almost ignorant that there
is an outside world; (b) the Kru tribes of the coast, who
know the white man; ambitious and energetic, they are

pagans, or Christian converts from paganism; (c) the Vai, Mandingo and the like — Mohammedans, independent and enterprising, traders by instinct. These three groups present three quite different problems to the government of the Liberian Republic. Far out-numbering the Americo-Liberians, better adapted to their surroundings, they must be utilized and assimilated or they will destroy. Properly utilized they will become the strength and bulwark of the nation. The group which presses and must most immediately play a significant part in Liberian affairs is that which includes the Vai. There are writers who demand that Liberia produce an actual African state. Delafosse, who as French consul lived in Monrovia and well knows the native populations criticizes the Liberians for too closely copying us. He believes they should have developed the native culture, have founded a Negro nation, different from European types. His demand is unreasonable, impossible of realization. The story of Liberia's origin demonstrates the impossibility. Liberia had to repeat us, even in our errors, because she came from us, is of us. Had she tried to do what Delafosse suggests, she would long since have been suppressed by hostile and jealous European powers. They would not permit such a nation to continue for a year upon the West Coast of Africa. Liberia must play the game as other nations, white nations, play it — or get off the board. Yet the Republic would be better off and stronger if she learns some lessons of the natives, if she took some hints from them, if she absorbed and cultivated some things they have developed. Among all her natives, there are none superior to the Vai. If Liberia cultivates close and intimate re-

lations with them she must perforce be tinctured by them.
Their social life and culture will affect her. There
should be vitality and helpfulness in the contact.
In closing may I not say two words about our author?
Mr. Ellis was eight years in Liberia as Secretary of the
American Legation at Monrovia. He was a faithful and
competent official, giving good service. He has been
useful to Liberia since his return and his thoughtful and
valuable articles regarding Liberian conditions and affairs have done much to keep American interest alive
regarding the only republic in Africa. During the period
of his service in Africa, Mr. Ellis found time and occasion to pursue the studies, the results of which are here
presented. Consuls and diplomatic officers have exceptional opportunities to enrich our knowledge of other
lands and peoples. Many such officials — British,
French, German, Russian — have made important contributions of that sort. American officials who have
done so are surprisingly few. Mr. Ellis sets an example
that is worthy of wide imitation.
Mr. Ellis is the third colored man to make conspicu-
ous contribution to the knowledge of conditions and
peoples in the Liberian region. The name of Edward
W. Blyden is known everywhere; his views upon social,
political, religious and race matters of West Africa command respect; his "Christianity, Islam and the Negro
Race" startled and instructed. Alexander Crummell
did a great work as man and educator in two continents;
his "Future of Africa" and "Africa and America" will
long be read with profit and delight. Neither of them
have gone into quite the field which Mr. Ellis enters.
But his "Negro Culture in West Africa" deserves a

place upon our shelves alongside of the well known books of those famous men. As a scientific investigation, as a contribution to social problems, as a basis for political action, it has a definite mission.

FREDERICK STARR.

CHICAGO, June 20, 1914.

PREFACE

The view entertained of the Negro African abroad is largely conditioned upon the knowledge possessed of the Negro in Africa. In this thought then the present study may have some bearing upon the interracial understanding between what is considered the two most divergent and dissimilar ethnic groups. The writer of the present volume went to West Africa to study the Negro African and his social conditions with Minister J. R. A. Crossland, who was appointed American Minister Resident and Consul General to the Republic of Liberia, in December, 1901, and continued his studies for nine years until about May, 1910, when he finally returned to the United States.

During the administration of Minister Ernest Lyon, which began in July, 1903, the American Legation at Monrovia, Liberia, took more interest in native affairs, perhaps, than had ever been taken before. Besides my special studies numerous official trips were taken into the far interior under instructions from Washington to report upon the various tribes and the facts surrounding the interior Anglo and Franco-Liberian boundaries, from the Mano River on the northwest to the Kavalla on the southeast; so, that on numerous occasions private studies coincided with official duties.

After going over much of the literature of West Africa and making some studies of the Dé, Gola, p esi, Basa, Grebo, Kru, Mende, Kondo, Gbandi, Mandingo,

Vai and other West African tribes, the conclusion was reached that the field was so large and the work so difficult, that in order to think of accomplishing anything worth while, it was necessary to select some particular group as a key to the African social situation, and to examine it as exhaustively as possible.

The Vais were chosen because they belong to the Mánde family, one of the most important and representative of the many ethnic divisions of the African Black Belt, numbering among its members the Landogho, Kondo, Gbandi, Mende, Soso, Bambara, Mandingo and Vai-speaking peoples. In addition to what obtained in the character and culture of other tribes, the Vais had a written national orthography, invented independently by themselves, and besides Arabic used by their upper and lettered classes.

The writer employed Vai scholars to instruct him in the Vai language and at times not occupied with his official duties as Secretary of the Legation, or Chargé d'Affaires ad interim, he visited the Vai people, travelling across their country, during the different expressions of their social activities; cultivated the most intimate acquaintance in frequent conferences with Vai savants and elders; secured specimens of their arts, representative of the various phases of their social life, and deposited them in the National Museum at Washington, D. C.; collected proverbs and folklore stories, and during nine years, embodied the results of his studies and the interpretations of Vai data in a manuscript under the title of " Negro Culture in West Africa."

Having taken courses in economics and sociology and philosophy and psychology the writer began this study chiefly to extend his information along sociological

lines; but the work soon became so engrossing that he
was carried beyond his original intentions. Much of
the information which he had obtained concerning the
Negro in Africa found in encyclopedias, geographies,
and works on ethnology and anthropology, was disclosed
to be unsupported by the facts as well as the general
picture of the intellectual and social condition of the
Negro in Africa, which has been so deeply impressed upon
the outside world.

His studies in West Africa revealed a Negro substantially different to what for the most part is described
in modern science and literature. Science had hitherto
in the main been compelled to rely upon the reports and
data supplied by transient travellers and resident visitors
who little understood African mentality, institutions and
society. But with the partition of Africa by European
powers there came into existence an increasing body of
European administrators and capable resident students
who began to describe to the world the Negro African,
something more like what he really is.

And as eminent and necessary as are the important
services rendered to science and the Negro by such distinguished Caucasian writers as Sir Harry H. Johnston, K.C.M.G., K.C.B., Sir A. B. Ellis, Mary H.
Kingsley, Lady Lugard, Dr. J. Scott Keltie, Count de
Cardi, E. D. Morel, Dr. Robert H. Nassau and M. Felix
DuBois, to the present writer it seems more necessary
and imperative, that the Negro should explain his own
culture and interpret his own thought and soul life, if
the complete truth is to be given to the other races of the
earth.

Blyden, Hayford and Sarbah have blazed the way
in West Africa; in Europe Tanner, Pushkin and Cole-

ridge-Taylor have taken their rank among the celebrities in painting, poetry and music; while in America DuBois, Dunbar, Ferris, Miller and Washington have indicated in literature and education the services which the Negro everywhere must render to himself and the Caucasian, if he is to contribute his proper portion toward the ultimate concord and cooperation of the races in the great upward trend of social progress. Should there be any justification, therefore, for the publication of the following manuscript, it is thought to be rather in the principle for which it stands than in the pride and glory of achievement.

The writer wishes to acknowledge his grateful thanks and appreciation to the members of the Kansas Congressional Delegation, and especially to the Honorables Charles F. Scott, Charles Curtis, Chester I. Long, and J. D. Bowersock, for their continuous encouragement and support while on the field.

For the high consideration and favor of Prof. Frederick Starr in writing the introduction, he is particularly gratified and grateful, not only because Prof. Starr is eminent as a scholar and anthropologist, but because of his travels in West Africa and his special knowledge of interior and tribal conditions in Liberian and Sierra Leone hinterlands.

He wishes finally to acknowledge his indebtedness to the numerous Vai and West African Negro scholars and thinkers, who contributed toward the work of the present volume, and above them all to his noted teacher and friend, Mormoru Duclay.

GEORGE W. ELLIS,
3262 Vernon Avenue,
Chicago, Illinois.

June 18, 1914.

NEGRO CULTURE IN WEST AFRICA

CHAPTER I

THE RELATION OF THE VAI TO THE NEGRO

THE Vai is one of the most interesting tribes in all Africa. It would be interesting if for no other reason than that, of the millions of Negroes of innumerable tribes, it has the distinction of being the only one that has a national orthography. Ethnologically the Vais belong to the Mánde Branch of the Negro race;[1] they are very closely related to the Soso, Bambara, and Mandingo peoples, and, like them, speak a branch of the Mánde tongue.[2] This family of the Negro race occupies the western part of High Sudan, between the 8th and 16th degrees of northern latitude and extending as far east as Timbuctu. Between Senegambia and Cape Palmas a narrow strip of lowland separates High Sudan from the Atlantic. The Mánde family extends into this lowland only at two points,— one in the Mánde territory, the other in the country of the Vais. The tribes of this lowland speak varied languages, entirely different from the Mánde,

[1] "Outlines of a Grammar of the Vai Language," by S. W. Koelle, p. 11, London, 1854; " The Races of Man and Their Geographical Distribution," by Oscar Peschel, p. 466, London, 1876.

[2] Máude and Mandingo, from same root manatus, meaning that the people worship this creature, a fish-god of the Songhays. Binger. E. D. Morel's "Affairs of West Africa," p. 211.

among which might be mentioned the Basá,   p esi,[3]
Kirim, Nálu, Fúlup, Timne, Baga, Balánta, Búlom, and
others.

THE VAI COUNTRY A PORTION OF THE GREAT NEGROLAND

The Vai country is a portion of the great Negroland,
which is inhabited by an estimated population of more
than thirty million Negroes. This Negroland was known
among ancient geographers by different names,— sometimes as Sudan, Ethiopia, Nigretia, and Tekrour, but
more generally as Genewah, from which we have derived the word Guinea. The Land of the Blacks, now
generally known as the Sudan, is a broad strip of territory, between the 7th and 17th parallels north latitude,
extending across the African continent from the Atlantic
to the southern mouth of the Red Sea, and marked by
a water belt of rivers and lakes from the Senegal to the
sources of the Nile. Along the northern limits of the
Sudan is the great desert of Sahara, beyond which lies
the fertile strip along the Mediterranean, occupied by the
Berber states. Connecting this fertile land of the north
and the Negro belt is the valley of the Nile, which suggests the possible influences long exercised upon the Negro
peoples.

OUTSIDE INFLUENCES UPON NEGROLAND

The Land of the Blacks was influenced by two great
forces, one from Egypt and the other from the Arabs
who conquered Spain,— which met each other in what

[3] Generally spelled Pessy. This spelling is according to the system accepted in London for the spelling of African names. See
article on "Liberia" in the *Geographical Journal* for August, 1905,
by Sir Harry Johnston, K.C.M.G., K.C.B.

is now known as Nigeria. In this vicinity the practice of embalming the dead was practised until early in modern times. The eastern end of Negroland has the alphabet of Egypt and Arabia, while the western has that of Morocco. The decorative art of the Hausa States bears a strong resemblance to that of Egypt; the town of Burrum had a tradition, at the time it was visited by Dr. Barth, that it had once been the habitation of the Pharaohs, and an Arab writer, by the name of Es Sardi, in his history of the Sudan, states that Kuka was at one time under the Pharaohs.

We know that the Phœnicians settled in North Africa, and keeping in close touch with Egypt, carried their conquest as far south as the Senegal, where they set up a kingdom over which Es Sardi states that twenty-two white kings reigned before the Hegira. Several nations, — among which were the Persians, Greeks, Romans, and Arabs,— in turn conquered Egypt and pressed upon the occupants of the northern states. The result of all this pressure upon the white people of that fertile strip that fringed northern Africa was that many of these people were driven into the desert, and later pressed upon the Negro peoples of Sudan. These outside influences had two main roads across the desert,— one through Tripoli, and one through Morocco. And through them poured all those Egyptian and Arabic forces that gave rise to these powerful Negro kingdoms in the Sudan, known as the Ghana, Melle, Songhay, Hausa, and Bornu kingdoms. Being rich in amber, gums, skins, cotton, gold, and other raw materials, for 800 years they flourished in turn, and with Europe and Asia carried on extensive trade across the desert waste. They were very powerful, and some of them had a standing army of upward of 200,000 soldiers, with 40,000 picked archers. To Ghana were tributary twenty Negro kingdoms and the white Berber state of Audaghost. Some of the kings,— possessing two capitals, and living in fortified castles that had glass windows and were decorated with sculptures and paintings,— had pageantries of the most stately magnificence. Indeed, when England, Germany, and France were just emerging from barbarism in intellectual, scientific, industrial, and political development, some of these dynasties had attained a comparatively high degree of civilization; and geographers and historians mention Ghana, Timbuctu, and other interior towns as the resorts for the rich, the learned, and the pious of all countries.[4]

Just as the white Africans of the fertile strip of the north pressed upon and influenced the Negroes all along the belt of Negroland, so the Negroes thus influenced pressed upon the Negroes toward the coast and south, and gave to many of them a great deal that they themselves had received through Arabic and Egyptian channels. As could only be expected, the finer Negro tribes are those that inhabit the northern portions of the great Sudan, and even to this day their teachers and scholars are influencing the pagan tribes nearer the coast. The Vai tribe is one of the few tribes that has pressed to the coast, with the evidences that it has been very much influenced

---

[4] Chief authorities for Introduction: Es Sardi, "History of Sudan"; Second Book of Herodotus; M. Dubois, "Timbuctu, the Mysterious"; "Historical Account of the Kingdom of Tek-rour, Denham, and Clapperton"; Dr. Barth's "Travels in Central Africa"; Lady Lugard's "West African Negroland" and "Journal of the Royal Colonial Institute"; "West African Studies," by M. H. Kingsley; "Affairs of West Africa," by E. D. Morel.

by the finer Negroes of the interior, especially in the matter of religious faith.[5]

THE ORIGIN OF THE VAIS

Whence came the Vais is a question to which I have received no conclusive answer. It is hardly probable that they have always remained on the coast where they are now,— in a country that extends from the coast several days' walk into the interior, and from about fifteen or twenty miles north of Monrovia, near Little Cape Mount, stretching northward to and including the Gallinas. It was in the latter section that the Rev. Koelle was informed in 1851 that about twenty years before that time the Spanish slave-traders had instigated the chiefs of the Vais to increase their territory to the limits then existing.[6]

In the interesting little book entitled " From the Darkness of Africa to the Light of America," published about 1890, Mr. Thomas E. Beselow, a Vai prince,— then a student at the Wesleyan Academy, Wilbraham, Massachusetts, and now living at Grand Cape Mount, Liberia,— gives the following account of the origin of the Vais: " More than two centuries ago a nomad tribe, numbering hundreds of men and women, left Abyssinia and for many years wandered toward the country west of the central part of Africa, like the Helvetians in the time of Cæsar. At last they arrived at a pleasant territory a little northeast of what is now the Republic of Liberia, and being pleased with the lay of the land concluded to

[5] Chief authorities for Introduction continued: "Christianity, Islam, and the Negro Race," by Dr. E. W. Blyden; "Intellectual Development of Europe," by J. W. Draper; Works of A. B. Ellis, 3 volumes: "Yoruba, Ewe, and Tshi Speaking Peoples."

[6] Vai Grammar, by the Rev. S. W. Koelle, Preface, p. iii, before mentioned.

make it their home and cease their wandering. This country was already occupied by a powerful tribe called the Gora." [7]

Mr. Beselow informs his reader that his mother told him this origin of the Vais, and he makes no attempt to prove that they came from Abyssinia only about two hundred years before. Later he gives as a reason for their long journey westward that he had heard it said " that it was to escape the iron rule of a tyrannical ruler." But it is hardly probable that a tribe so small as the Vai made such a long journey through powerful states without being reduced to bondage, and it would have been very difficult for the Vais to reach their present abode without passing through the great Bornu and Hausa kingdoms. Moreover, there is nothing pointed out in the language, institutions, and ethnography of the Vais and Abyssinians even to suggest an assumption of a common origin; and in view of the ethnological relation of the Vais to the Mandingoes, Bambaras, and other tribes,— to none of which any reference has been made, at least for the present,— the theory of the Abyssinian origin of the Vais must be regarded as highly improbable.

The Rev. Koelle, who visited the Vai country about 1851 and wrote a Vai grammar, gives as his opinion that the Vais came from the interior.[8]   This belief he based on the fact that on the north and south of the Vais lived people who spoke entirely different languages from theirs; the Kirim was spoken on the north, and the relics of the Déwoi on the south, and other tribes have pushed to the coast to secure the commercial advantages thereof.

---

[7] "From the Darkness of Africa to the Light of America," by T. E. Beselow, p. 22. Gora is usually spelled Gola or Golah.

[8] "Vai Grammar," by the Rev. S. W. Koelle, Preface, p. iii.

Moreover, he found a tradition among the Vai people themselves "that they emigrated from a district of the Mánde country." He thought that the emigration had taken place about two hundred years before 1851, on account of the changes in the language, but not later than a hundred years, allowing for language differences that might have existed before the emigration. He thought also that the Mándes,— who, tradition says, were under the command of Fábule and Kiatamba,[9]— not only took the country but adopted the name of the conquered people.[10]

From what I learned in a trip across a portion of the Vai country, I think the opinion expressed by the Rev. Koelle is highly probable. At Grand Cape Mount there is a lake called Peso [11] extending twenty-five or thirty miles into the interior, and I went to the end of it, stopping at the important towns, among which was Dátia,— mentioned by the Rev. Koelle,— and after a few days' journey into the interior I walked about a hundred miles across the Vai country to Monrovia. I was informed by numerous chiefs that the Vais came from the Mandingo country under the leadership not only of Fábule and Kiatamba, but of Cassu and Manobá, his son. A story was told to

[9] The spear which Kiatamba brought with him is said to be now at Bomie, a town in the Vai country. I was at this town when the king died.

[10] There is a Mandingo word, andavai, meaning split from, and it is very likely that the word Vai is derived from it. I was informed by a Vai scholar that when the people now called Vais separated from the Mandingoes the remaining Mandingoes called those who left Vais, as an appropriate name on account of their action in separating from the main branch of the tribe. It is said that the separation was caused by the dissatisfaction of rival brothers contending for the Mandingan throne.

[11] From Mandingo Peling-So, meaning dove-pond, a small basin of water in which the doves washed. It is now a large lake.

me to the effect that a Mandingo king of Musardu had a son who broke a law which, according to custom, forfeited his life, and that his father, who dearly loved him, to save his life escaped with him and a number of his followers, who made their way to the Tegyá country and founded the Vai tribe. From this tradition it seems that Vai was not the name of the country subdued as was suggested by the Rev. Koelle; yet in essential points the traditions mentioned by him and the one told to me agree, except that the latter is somewhat more explicit. Whether it be true or not, it has the merit of being both possible and probable.

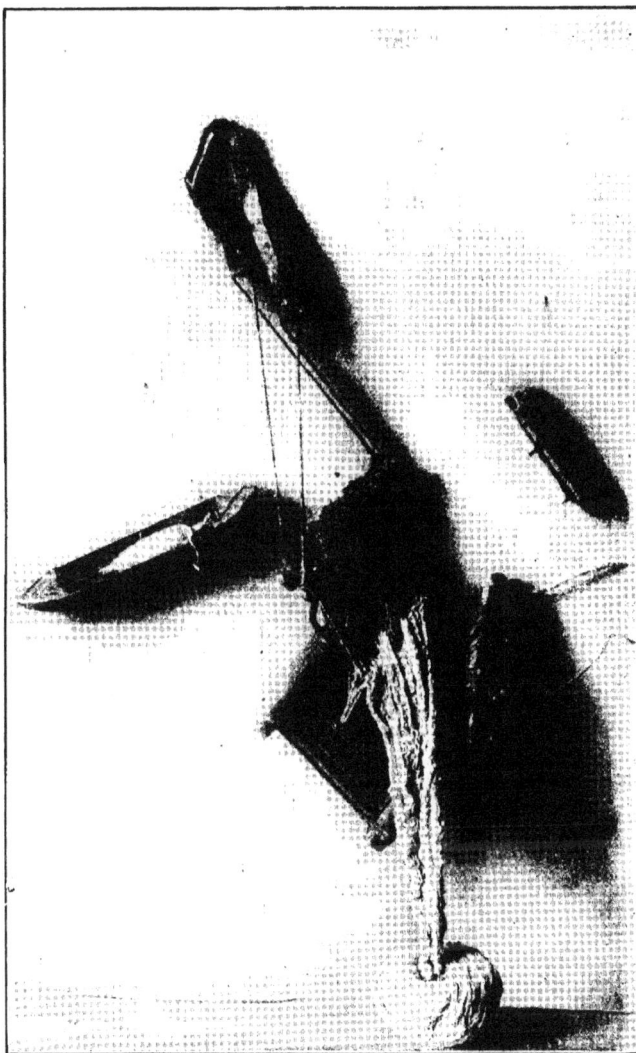

VAI MACHINE FOR WEAVING CLOTH

Facing Page 28

CHAPTER II

SOME PHYSICAL ASPECTS OF THE VAIS

PERSONAL FEATURES, SIZE, COLOR, EYES, AND HAIR

THE Vais are generally known to possess fairly good personal features, some of the men being handsome, splendid in physique, and intelligent in bearing. They have neither the strength and physical endurance of the p esi nor the stalwart frames of the Krus, yet they are not pigmies, but medium in size. The women are attractively developed and possess charms above all their sisters of the Gora, p esi, Bandi, Basa, Bere,[1] Kru, and other Liberian tribes. And some of them are very beautiful. At Dátia I saw a young Vai maid of seventeen, who was so pleasing in her personal appearance that because of her beauty she was without doubt the belle of that town. She had just come from the "Greegree Bush," and was said to be betrothed to the son of the chief. There were many other good-looking Vai girls and women, which goes to show that personal beauty is a thing monopolized by no particular people.

In color the Vais range from dark olive to coal black. The skin of the better classes of the Vais is smooth and velvety, while that of the lower classes is somewhat coarse and rough. On some of them I examined the skin that had been exposed to the sun and that that had not been so exposed. The parts affected by the sun seemed

[1] Sometimes spelled Bele.

darker and less oily than unexposed portions, and under the clothes of some of them I noticed little spots that were lighter in color.   The body of the lower classes is almost entirely unclad, so only on a portion of the thigh and under the arm could I find places not habitually exposed to the sun, and the skin under the clothes is soft and oily in appearance and much lighter than in other places.   Persons black in the face were brown in unexposed portions of the body or arm.   The feet, being exposed to the weather, are often positively sooty and rough; yet the small, neat, smooth feet of many Vais naturally attracted attention and excited comment in the Vai country, and they may be seen any time in the Vai towns in the outer limits of Monrovia.

The eyes of the Vais, so far as I have been able to observe, range from black-brown in the color of the iris to dark hazel and what is called the neutral eye, the exact color of which cannot be distinguished at once.   The position of the eyes in the head is similar to that of Europeans, the long axis being substantially in one horizontal plane.   The eye is medium in size and usually has a frank and pleasant appearance.   Now and then among the Vais one may see a Mongolian eye, with its compressed and outer angles, but this is very rare.

The hair of the Vais differs very much in its quality, from the woolly to the undulating and wavy.   It is usually black in color, and the better quality is more generally observed among the women, some of whom have hair in abundance and of great beauty.   The hair of infants is of a brownish color, sometimes very light, and grows darker as the child advances in years.   As a general thing the Vais have the hair uniformly distributed over the head, though the quantity possessed is usually moderate.   The young men keep their hair cut very close, and the women have theirs long enough to be arranged according to their custom,— which does not require it to be very long. The Vai men have some beard, but not a great deal; and many of them have hair on their breasts, while both sexes have it in the armpits and on the pubes. Baldness is not commonly observed among the Vais, though now and then one will see very old men who are bald. The Vais and the Mandingoes shave the heads of the boys and young men, and if this has been practised for any length of time, it may be that this custom has had a tendency to strengthen the hair.

The faces of the Vais are generally medium in size; some of them are short and broad while others are long and narrow, and now and then you will find one narrowing upward or toward the chin. The Vais have the Negroid nose, but the openings are not so large nor the nose so flat as in the case of the typical Negro. Among them, of course, may be found great varieties of noses, ranging between the Negroid and the straight; some of them are as represented in the Negro type, but this is not the rule. The lips, like the nose of the Vais, are not as shown in the Negro type, but are medium in size, with a slight turn to the upper and lower lips.[2]   And notwithstanding their custom of going barefooted, their feet are usually fairly well shaped, and sometimes even noticeably small and well shaped.

THE ACCEPTED NEGRO TYPE

"The typical Negro is a rare variety even among Negroes,"

[2] "The thin lips of the European and their American descendants are a character that brings them nearer the monkeys."— Oscar Peschel.

says Winwood Reade.[3] I have found this strikingly true among the Vais. In fact I have been able to see so little of the Negro type even among other tribes of West Africa that I have wondered how any ethnologist with a modicum of information of any African tribe could ever have given to the world such a cruel misrepresentation as is embodied in the Negro type. Mr. Peschel calls them mistaken ethnologists, and gives their opinion of the Negro in these words:

" The Negro was the ideal of everything barbarous and beastlike. They endeavored to deny him any capability of improvement, and even disputed his position as a man. The Negro was said to have an oval skull, a flat forehead, snoutlike jaws, swollen lips, a broad flat nose, short crimped' hair, falsely called wool, long arms, meager thighs, and flat feet. No single tribe, however, possesses all these deformities." [4]

At the time this Negro type, so graphically described by Mr. Peschel, was sent forth, with this seal of science and impressed upon the world, great nations were robbing Africa of her sons and dooming them to pitiless lives of unrequited toil. The consciences of kings and nations alike were lulled to sleep by the love and hope of gain. But human slavery was so cruel in itself, so repugnant to the natural rights of man, that its continuance in time necessitated the sanction and authority of science. As

[3] " Savage Africa," by Winwood Reade, p. 516.
[4] " Races of Mankind," by Oscar Peschel, p. 463. Dr. Anson P. Atterbury in his " Muhammudanism in Africa," although he is just and liberal in many respects, gives a similar picture of the Negro type,—a picture that can be found only in the imagination of those unacquainted with the Africans, p. 49.

slavery grew and was extended, its evils grew and were multiplied. There was consequently then an ever increasing demand for ethnologists to create a Negro type that was false, barbarous, and beast-like,— one that represented the Negro as incapable of all improvement, and which would strengthen the sentiment that sought to bar the Negro from the human race. It is not necessary to say that the type born of this slave sentiment fully met the demand, for it contained about all the deformities possible to a human being and has done incalculable harm to the Negro race.

This false Negro type was set forth in encyclopædias, represented in geographies, and described in works of ethnology and other books with ethnic features. It would be as unjust to say that there were no Negroes corresponding to this type as it would be to contend that such creatures are typical of the race; for there are some Negroes in every tribe whom this type hardly misrepresents. Every lover of the truth desires,— and it is due to the Negro race,— that his features, character, and institutions be truthfully represented. Until it has been proved that the majority of the Negro peoples conform to the present accepted Negro type, in the interest of truth and ethnological science, the false Negro type should be changed to conform to the simple facts.[5] The tribes of Africa are being studied now as they have never been studied before. Since Miss Mary Kingsley ceased her valuable contributions to the studies of African peoples many valuable books have been published concerning the life and institutions of African tribes, among which I might mention the works of Sir A. B. Ellis, E. D. Morel,

[5] "Redemption of Africa," by F. P. Noble, p. 166; "Races of Man," by Oscar Peschel, p. 464.

Sir Harry Johnston, Casely Hayford,[6] John M. Sarbah, a native African, and the many writings of Dr. Edward W. Blyden, the eminent writer and sage of West Africa. The African is gradually being represented to the world as he really is. Mr. Benjamin Kid, a noted writer and author, says that the economic center of the world is slowly shifting toward the tropics.[7] If this be true, interest in Africa and Africans will increase with the years, and it is only a question of time when, to harmonize with the truth, the accepted Negro type must be changed.

INFLUENCES OF CLIMATE IN WEST AFRICA

West Africa has the reputation of having one of the worst, if not the worst, climate in the world. Since it acquired this reputation, however, many forces have been introduced for the improvement of West Africa, so that while the climate is still bad enough it is hardly as bad as it is reputed to be. You will find in the encyclopædias that West Africa is still referred to as " the white man's grave." There is no doubt that the climate of West Africa is very severe. It is no respecter of persons, and the African suffers as well as people from the temperate zone; but having been accustomed to centuries of exposure the African suffers less than do the members of other races. The natural effect of the climate in West Africa is to enfeeble both the body and the intellect. Young men often come to West Africa strong and stalwart, but if they do not die they soon find their health seriously impaired by the malaria which lurks in the

[6] Also a native African.
[7] The *Independent,* September 8, 1904, an article by Benjamin Kid.

wooded lowlands along the coast.   A residence in West
Africa necessitates taking medicine almost constantly, and
then the man that takes it seems to fare little better than
the rest.   As you go interiorward the climate becomes
more healthful.

Europeans have been unable, as yet, to colonize to any
great extent in West Africa.   And the death rate is still
high among those who go there for commercial or political considerations, though they seldom remain longer than
a year, with a leave of six months on the continent.
Among the natives many diseases may be found that are
apparently peculiar to them and the climate.   And just as
the climate of West Africa, so inimical to man, enfeebles
the body, it preys upon the mind.[8]   Its effect upon the
memory is so noticeably bad that you often hear persons
apologizing for having acquired a " West African memory."

The effect upon the will is quite as well known as that
upon the memory.   Persons coming from abroad find
Africa very slow; they have determined to do many
things; they criticise everything and everybody, and ask
why Africans do not move about briskly.   After having
been in Africa for years they find that their plans do not
materialize.   In a little while they cease to criticise, and
later they take on the African movement.   There is something in the climate that makes any kind of work extremely irksome.   In West Africa the body loses its
strength, the memory its retentiveness, and the will its
energy.   These are the effects observed upon persons remaining in West Africa only for a short time, and they
form a part of the experience of almost every person who

[8] " The Tshi Speaking Peoples," by Sir A. B. Ellis, p. 4.

has lived on the West Coast. White persons,— with beautiful skin, clear and soft, and with rosy cheeks,— after they have been in West Africa for a while become dark and tawny like the inhabitants of southern Spain and Italy.[9] If we can detect these effects of the West African climate in only a short time upon persons who come to the West Coast, what must have been the effect of such a climate upon the Negroes who for centuries have been exposed to its hardships?

DECORATION AND DRESS

In his admirable essay on education Mr. Herbert Spencer remarks that " Decoration always precedes dress." This truth is strikingly illustrated among the backward peoples. Yet there is not a great deal of decoration used by the tribes in Liberia. The members of the Kru tribes have tattooing on their faces, consisting of a blue mark in the center of the forehead running toward the nose, a blue triangle in each temple, and other marks on the arms. But the tendency thus to disfigure themselves is dying out. There is no decline in the use of clay, however, and it may be frequently seen in varied colors in Monrovia.

Among the Vais I noticed on the body of the boys who had been in the Devil Bush two stripes, or rows, tattooed down the back and around the waist to the side. These rows were not colored, but were the simple scars which had been made by cutting. Girls from the Greegree Bush had across the small of the back a rectangle, artistically cut without coloring, and in size about three inches by eight.

[9] Negroes from America and the West Indies fare but little if any better than the Europeans. Miss Kingsley says " that the descendants of the exported Africans have seemingly lost their power of resistance to the malarial West Coast climate." " West African Studies," by M. H. Kingsley, p. 53.

Other than the foregoing on the persons of the Vais I have seen no permanent marks.

Decoration in the way of ornaments depends largely upon the wealth and standing of the wearer. The better class of men wear rings of silver or gold, silver and gold armlets and anklets, small deer horns ornamented with silver or gold, and various amulets of a religious import with gold or silver bands. Men of less means wear the same ornaments, but of less costly material. I have noticed some with iron and copper and brass anklets.

Boys generally go unclad until they are ten or eleven years old, when according to station they wear a simple cloth tied about the loins or a short gown. The boys from the Devil Bush and the girls from the Greegree Bush, in honor of their coming out, wear various kinds of jewelry, beads, rings, horns, and silver breastplates. As a sign of virginity the girls wear beads about the hips and a very small horn suspended from the neck, containing medicine which it is said will kill any person who violates the person of the wearer. There are other signs, too; but of whatever nature they may be they are worn until marriage. White clay is used by the girls in the Greegree Bush, and those who are betrothed use brown clay, which is made from the fat of animals mixed with perfume and olives. There is another kind of clay that is usually worn by women at night, and which is highly scented with the bark of a tree. I ascertained that clay is used among the Vais for three purposes,— for decoration, for protection to the skin, and as a medicine. Women during pregnancy use it as a medicine, and I saw many of them with this clay spread thickly over the entire person. When used for decorative purposes alone, different kinds are put on in artistic combinations.

The ornaments of the king consist of his breastplate, rings, anklets, horns, and various armlets, all especially made for him. The king's ornaments are made of the best and most costly material to be had, and no one may wear any like his.

In the matter of dress the Vais and Mandingoes wear much more than do most of the tribes in Liberia. The boys and girls wear little or nothing until they are ten years old. Afterward the girls wear an apron made of beads, and the boys a breechcloth or gown. When the boys and girls come out of the Devil and Greegree Bushes they dress especially for the occasion. They have a full supply of clothes, with shoes and hats, besides beads, horns, leopard teeth, and various kinds of jewelry. The boys wear a silver breastplate, and the slaves are permitted to wear only one shoe. The men of the ordinary class among the Vais wear a cloth folded about over the breechcloth, while the gentlemen wear gowns or shirts and pants that are very loose and cut very much like those of the Chinaman. The quality of the goods varies with the taste and wealth of the wearers. The common woman wears two or more cloths folded about the waist, generally of country cloth or foreign-made goods, according to native fashion or taste. The more wealthy woman wears better and more cloth, and in addition a large silk handkerchief around the head and about the shoulders. Men of the best standing carry a whip on their shoulders as evidence thereof; and younger men have a custom of carrying as a part of their dress a silk handkerchief over their shoulders.

The Vai priests have a special dress which distinguishes them from the other people. They wear the best of clothes, according to Vai custom,— hat, shoes, and a long

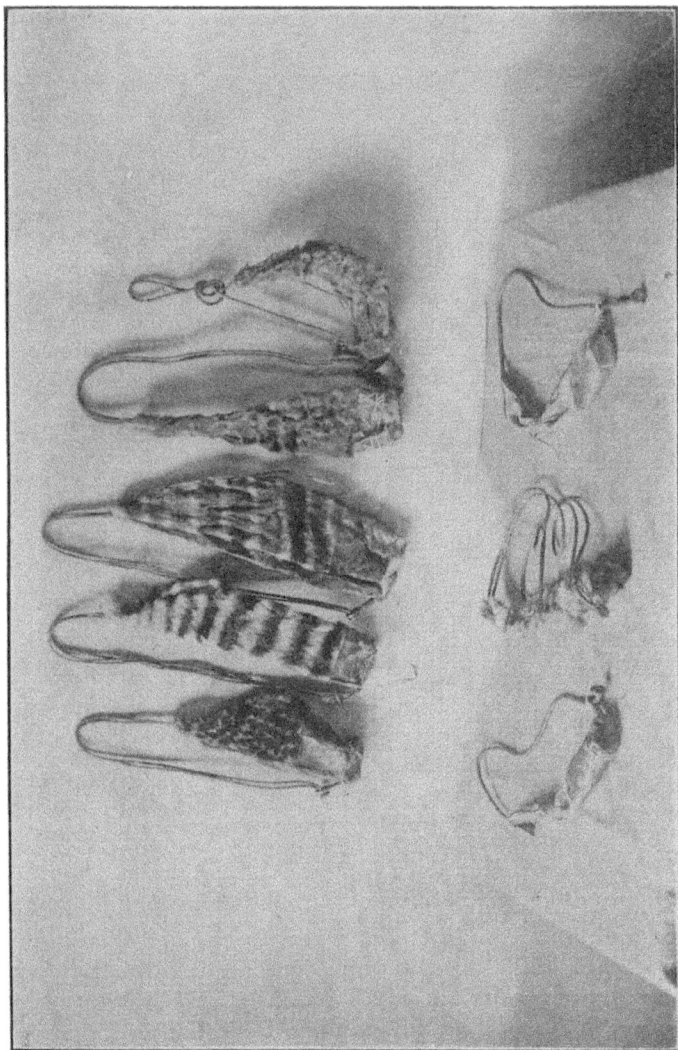

NATIVE BAGS FOR TRINKETS

white gown, with a long string of beads around the neck. There is a special dress for war. The common soldier wears a shirt and short pants, a leopard-skin cap, and is armed with gun or war-knife, and a few have axes. Each one has a small bag containing medicine from the doctor who presages good by cutting sand on a leopard hide. The dress of the chiefs is made almost entirely of leopard skins. The cap, shirt, and pants have sewed on them little bags of medicine covered with red flannel. On the sides of the cap, and on the sides and back of the leopard-skin garments, are rows of sea-shells. A strip of ram fur is sewed down the center and hangs down the back of the general's cap. Each chief wears a breastplate of silver, containing medicine from the doctor, ranging in value from $25 to $100.

The shoes of the king are made of the best leather, and his hats of the best cloth and grass. He has the finest gowns, pants, and country cloths made especially for him. In addition he has garments made of the skins of various animals like the leopard, with the best native trimmings. The king's most attractive dress consists of his coronation robes of scarlet cloth, and those which he selects to wear on ceremonial occasions when he is attended by all his important chiefs and warriors. The king has the most costly breastplate, beautifully carved, with a compartment in the center for the god of defense and his country medicine. He has a full supply of all the weapons of war, carved and ornamented with the rarest native decorations and designs.

CHAPTER III

ECONOMIC LIFE OF THE VAIS

IMPORTANCE OF AGRICULTURE AND CULTIVATED PRODUCTS

AGRICULTURE is the main dependence of the Vais,
— in fact, of most of the tribes in Liberia. The
products cultivated are cotton, rice, cassava,[1] Kaffir seed,
corn, eddoes, pumpkins, pattoes, okrá, potatoes, oats,
bananas, oranges, plantains, lemons, limes, pawpaws,
ground peas, ginger, and coffee. The head of the family
has a farm, or farms. Every free young man must have
a rice farm. The farming is very simple. The Vais
possess servants consisting of captives taken in war and
boys and girls secured from neighboring tribes for fifteen
or twenty dollars in trade goods. The Vai men of high
standing or wealth have their male servants to cut their
farms in February and March during the drys; and when
the underbrush and timber are cut and burned the farm is
turned over to the female servants to plant in April. The
crops become ripe at different times during the year, but
the general harvest time is in June and July. Some of
the products are raised more than once during the year
and gathered in early drys. Those who are not able to
have servants of course do their own work. The same
farmland is only used once in six or seven years. The
Vais, on account of the prolificness of the soil, do little
more than barely scratch the ground.

[1] Also spelled cassada. In Liberia it is spelled cassada and is so
pronounced. Cassava is more widely known.

The land is supposed to belong to the whole tribe. The king and his council allot so much to each chief for the support of the towns and half-towns. The farms are generally near the half-towns. Individuals secure their farms from the chief of their section. As long as a man is cultivating a piece of land it belongs to him; but when he ceases to cultivate the soil it may be granted to some one else. Axes and cutlasses are employed in preparing the forest for burning, some of which implements are bought by the Vais near Liberian settlements, and others are made by their own workmen farther in the interior. The rice is scratched into the ground with a small hoe, African in design and make. After the clearing and burning of the farm the planting, working, and gathering of the crop are left to the female servants and the poorer classes of the Vai women.

THE CONSUMPTION OF NATURAL PRODUCTS

Aside from agricultural products the Vais have many native food materials, some of which are staple articles. I might mention such products as palm nuts, cola nuts, palm cabbage, wild yams, pineapples, walnuts, sherry, troes, palm wine, rusty and sour plums, monkey apples, spider groundnuts, and strawberries. The palm-tree is one of the most important trees in Africa. It is among the main supports of the native African. From this tree he gets palm wine, which is drunk a great deal by farm hands when working the farms. This wine when fresh is very pleasant and sweet, but when old is very intoxicating. It is usually procured in the morning. There are two methods,— one, to cut the tree down and tap the cabbage and allow the wine to drip into a basin; the other, to climb the tree, insert a tube in the cabbage, and catch the wine as it comes from the tube.

This cabbage containing the wine is also good to eat and is very much enjoyed among the native peoples. The palm bears from four to seven bunches of palm nuts per annum, which ripen generally during the drys. These nuts are covered with a layer of oily substance, from which palm oil and butter are made. The nut contains a large seed, the outside of which is used by the iron, silver, and goldsmiths for fuel; the inside, called the palm kernel, is shipped to Europe in large quantities from West Africa, and from it soap, oil, candles, and other articles are made. The branches of the tree are used for the covering of houses, and from certain other parts are made nets, baskets, mats, rice fanners, and other articles of domestic utility. In these palm-trees are certain large grugru worms, which are also eaten by the natives. The Kru-family are great people for making palm butter and rice, but their reputation can hardly be compared with that of the Vais for making palaver sauce.

The Vais raise domestic animals and fowls. In the interior I noticed among them cows, goats, sheep, and bullocks. I also saw geese, ducks, and chickens. With hooks, nets, and other devices they catch fish. With bows and arrows, and guns and various kinds of traps they hunt and catch the antelope, deer, wildcat, monkey, leopard, bushcow, elephant, and other animals. With their knives they attack, kill, and eat the boa-constrictor, and birds of the most gorgeous plumage fall captive to their hunting skill.

TRAFFIC AND THE ARTICLES THEREOF

Another factor in the economic life of the Vais is traffic. To secure larger commercial opportunities was no doubt one of the chief motives which led them to press to the coast line. They engage in trade with Europeans and Liberian merchants at Cape Mount; and formerly the Liberian settlement at Cape Mount had direct control of foreign trade. These Liberians constitute the most important factor in distributing foreign articles to neighboring tribes and in securing in return the products of West Africa. As soon as the rice season is over the Vais take up traffic among themselves and with their neighbors. Some of the articles which enter into this traffic are cotton goods, brass kettles, cap guns, sword blades, iron pots, crockery, powder, gin, salt, gun caps, tobacco, cheap jewelry, silk goods and other articles of like nature. In exchange for the above articles they secure rubber, piassava, cocoa, coffee, palm kernels, palm oil, ginger, and calabar beans, which constitute the principal articles for exportation from this part of West Africa. Vai traders, influenced by the profits of domestic and foreign traffic, penetrate far into the interior with their goods. Foreigners, as a rule, are not permitted to trade outside of the ports of entry, which gives to the natives a practical monopoly of the far interior trade.

PRODUCTS OF THE INDUSTRIAL ARTS

Perhaps the most interesting phase of Vai economic life is that which includes the products which represent Vai industrial skill. The remarkable similarity between the design and products of the Vais and Mandingoes is very good evidence of the close relation of the two tribes in the past. I have been very much interested in securing some of the products of Vai industrial art and skill. I might call your attention to just a few:

1. Knives, swords, and spears, with common leather cases.

2. Common and fancy snuff, and war horns made from ivory and bushcow, and other horns.

3. Fur-covered bags for trinkets, and so on, with leather ornamentations and round leather plaited straps.

4. Various fancy bags made of grass for carrying money, medicine, and trinkets.

5. Machine for weaving cotton cloth, made of wood and fiber.

6. Rope, common and fancy hammocks, made of grass and other materials.

7. Country hoes and cutlasses made from iron.

8. Plates, bowls, and pots made from clay.

9. Chairs, beds, and so on, made of bamboo, with caned bottoms.

10. Country shoes of wood and decorated leather.

11. Various kinds of drums made of wood and hides.

12. Various kinds of caps and hats made of grass and country cloth.

13. Country whips and symbols of authority made of leather and grass.

14. Common and fancy-colored cotton cloth in great varieties.

15. Spoons and plates and bowls made of wood, as well as canoes, mortars, and pestles.

16. Ink and dyes made from leaves and barks.

17. Rice fanners made of bamboo and other materials.

18. Trays for various games such as moh, otherwise called king's game.

I noticed also a number of musical instruments used in plays and dances and when the king goes on a visit to any of his chiefs.

1. The common drums consist of logs cut the desired length and thinly hollowed, with tanned hide stretched over one end and fastened with palm fiber.

2. The women have sasas, made of gourds covered with thread nets and with shells attached, which strike against the gourd when the sasa is shaken.

3. They have what they call king's drums, beaten by the king's musicians for the king's pleasure. They are made of small hollowed limbs with hide at both ends and strung around the sides, and they are seldom used except when the king is going out. These drums are carried under the arm and beaten with one stick made for the purpose.

4. They have an instrument made of a sheet of iron rolled so as to be left hollow, and this hollow part is held in the palm of the left hand; then there is an iron ring on the left thumb which is struck against the iron sheet after each beat made by a stick in the other hand.

5. They also have an instrument made of two small baskets containing round pebbles which are shaken, one in each hand.

6. Each king has a large war horn made of ivory and ornamented with silver or gold.

7. They have a gourd with holes made in it, which is blown and fingered like a fife. In war times they talk in this instrument and call the names of warriors.

8. I noticed an instrument made much in the shape of a ladder, with small sticks tied across two long bars, suspended beneath which were gourds diminishing in size.

The Vais living in closest proximity to Liberian settlements have almost entirely ceased to make very many of the various articles that I have mentioned, because they can easily buy for a small price many of them from Liberian and foreign merchants who have been supplied with these articles by Europeans who have studied the tastes and wants of the African. But as you proceed interiorward, more and more do you see the products which have been made by the skilled hands of the Vais.

CHAPTER IV

NATURE OF THE SOCIAL INSTITUTIONS OF
THE VAIS

SOCIAL CONDITIONS, TOWNS, HALF-TOWNS, AND HOUSES

LIKE the tribes on the West Coast of Africa, the Vais are distributed over a thickly wooded country of wild and tangled forests, the natural abode of poisonous reptiles and the nightly haunts of ferocious beasts. Here may be found the prowling leopard, the fierce crocodile, and the manlike chimpanzee. Here may be seen the elephant, the buffalo, the hippopotamus, and the cruel, dreaded boa-constrictor lying for days in ambush for its prey. This section is principally drained by the Mano, Máfá, and Little Cape Mount rivers. At Grand Cape Mount is a lovely lake extending for miles into the interior, and beside it is a range of hills the insular crest of which at the coast is 1065 feet above the level of the sea. For seven months there is almost continual rain, and for five months it is dry with transitions of intermittent showers. The climate is very damp during the rains and very warm during the drys. The mean average temperature at Monrovia is 83° F., with daily variations from 77° to 90°. Communication is slow and difficult, and to persons living away from rivers walking is the only way of traveling.

The Vai people are scattered over the Vai country in

towns and half-towns, which are connected with one another by narrow, winding foot-paths. The tendency is toward the social group. Here isolation would not only be unpleasant and inconvenient, but positively unsafe. Real African towns are the abodes of kings, past or present. In a town rice kitchens and the making of palm oil are prohibited. Towns are intended for comfort, pleasure, and the full enjoyment of the highest African life. But the half-towns are industrial,— the main source and center of securing sustenance. The sites of the towns and half-towns are selected usually in some healthy spot where water is easily obtained; the former, where it would be difficult of approach to an attacking foe; the latter, with reference to its convenience to the gardens and the farms. The towns are generally on hills, commanding wide views of the neighboring country, and surrounded with two or three walls of barricade twenty-five or thirty feet apart. On the sides of approach the ground is covered with large logs, at inconvenient distances apart, or with sharp sticks thickly stuck into the ground.

The towns are social, the half-towns economic, centers. In the latter are found the rice kitchens, the making of palm oil, the raising of domestic fowls and animals. The towns consist of individual houses generally grouped about an open space in the center and not far distant from one another, with thoroughfares running both ways. The houses are usually circular, with cone-shaped roofs and dirt floors thrown up three or four feet above the general level. The lower framework is selected from the varied timbers of the country and is covered on the outside with mud. The roofing is chiefly of palm branches. The houses of the half-towns are temporary structures and change frequently with the changing of the farms.

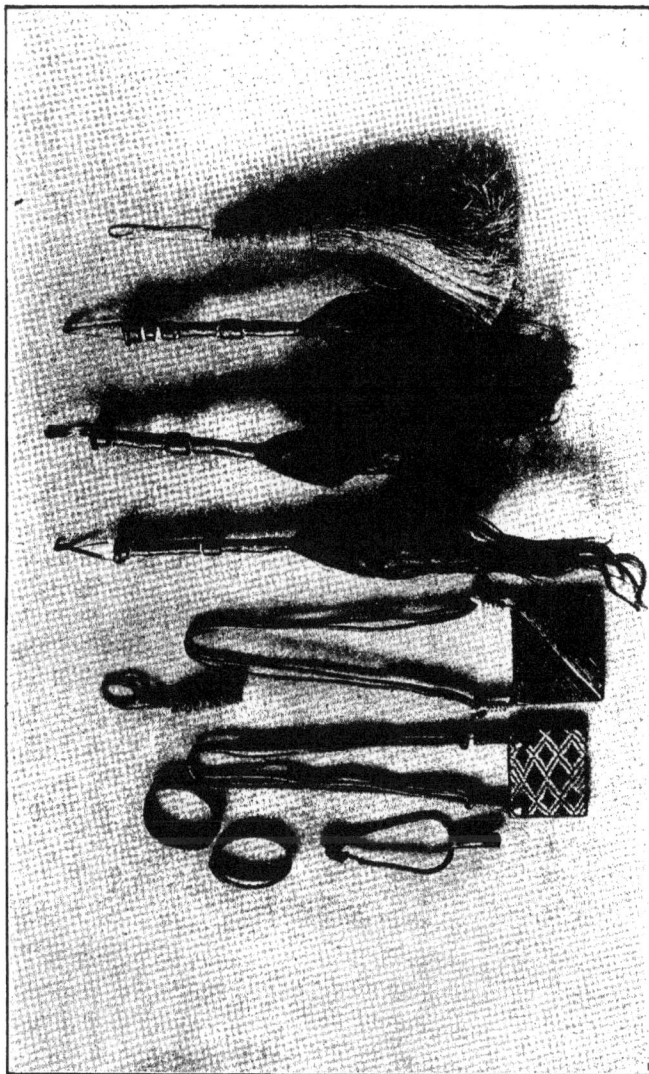

NATIVE FETICHES AND SYMBOLS OF AUTHORITY

The houses contain two rooms as a rule, and when there is more than one wife there is a house for each one. The kitchen is the place where are generally kept the pots, spoons, plates, rice fanners, cloth weavers, a few chairs, and a hammock. It has also a fire-hearth. In the other room, which is used for bedroom, are chairs and a bed of bamboo, wooden trunks, water pots made of clay, a rattan line or bamboo rack for the hanging up of clothes, country mats, and in some a fire-hearth. The towns of the Vais are kept very clean and the houses are noticeably superior to the houses of neighboring tribes.

AIM AND PRINCIPLES OF THE " DEVIL BUSH "

The " Devil Bush " is one of the most important social institutions of the Vais,— in fact, of most of the tribes in Liberia. It is but one of many whose social functions differ in form but whose general purposes are substantially the same. Among the various tribes it is known by different names, but its mission and purpose are always the same. It has been my observation that most of the social institutions of the natives ultimately tend to strengthen authority and to render government less difficult, and this is especially true of the " Devil Bush." The " Devil Bush " is a secret organization, and its operations are carried on in an unknown place. The penalty for divulging its secrets is said to be death. I know that it is very difficult to ascertain much information regarding it.

The head of the society is called a " Country Devil." He has sole power and is assisted by other members of the tribe versed in the principles of the organization. The society meets in what is called sessions, varying in duration from three to ten years. It admits only males that are between the ages of seven and fifty. When the organization is in session no one is allowed, under penalty of death, to visit the scene of its workings. The paramount aim of this society is to train young boys for African life. More definitely stated the boys are taught the industrial trades, native warfare, religious duties, tribal laws and customs, and the social arts.

Aside from the secrets of the society it has purely an educational purpose. In the application of its principles there is no respect of rank. The bow and arrow may be called the Vai alphabet. Every morning the small boys are taught first to use skilfully this weapon. In addition they are taught to throw the spear and to wield the sword. In the afternoon they are taken on a hunt for small game, and later are given practice in target shooting and throwing the spear. After supper the boys take up singing and dancing. At this period they are taught also their duties to the gods, to whom a certain portion of their meals is said to be offered. Each boy is taught the sacrificial ceremony; they all clap, dance, and sing their songs of praise.

When the boys have attained a certain advancement among other things they have sham battles, with 200 or 150 boys on a side. A district is given to one side to be captured by the other. Each side has a captain, and at this stage of their development emphasis is placed upon the display of bravery. And sometimes the contests assume aspects of reality. When one side repulses another six times it is said to be victorious. They are next taught the actual methods employed in the higher phases of native warfare. The most difficult feat in native warfare is the taking of strongly fortified and barricaded towns. Where the town to be taken is defended with powder and shot, the attacking party builds a barricade around the town to cut off its water and other supplies. When thus weakened the town is attacked. If repulsed, they re-attack the town and storm the barricades on a dark and rainy night when the loud thundering renders their approach unheard.

Besides teaching the above method of taking towns another is taught. The attacking party is arranged around a town,— four or five miles distant. A small band is sent to make the attack, with the understanding that they are to pretend to be frightened and flee. It is supposed that the smallness of their numbers will entice the warriors of the town to follow; who, having come out a certain distance, are surrounded and taken by an unexpected force.

And still another method of attack is taught. A man, as a friend, is sent into the town desired to be taken. Sometimes more than one are sent. Late at night, when everybody has retired except those on guard at the gates, these emissaries kill the sentinel at a certain gate and permit the attacking army to enter the town without the warning of the guards. Each man is supposed to take a house, and when the various warriors have seized the supplies and are ready for battle the war cry is sounded, and as the men of the town are fleeing for safety, amid the roar and excitement of the hour, they are pierced with spears and cut to pieces with swords wielded by warriors from unexpected quarters. 'Tis quite natural in such a confused contest in the dark that some women and children should be killed, but the custom is to spare them. The leaders who escape death are afterwards executed; the women, men, and children are held as slaves. And generally the town is burned to the ground.

In addition to being taught the methods of warfare, the

boys are taught the civil and military laws governing the
Vai people. Every Vai man must know the law. And as
the penalties for violating the laws covering military ex-
peditions are so severe, the customs and laws relating
thereto are of paramount importance to every Vai man.
The king is commander-in-chief of the army. He seldom
accompanies his army. It is commanded either by the
general or a trusted chief. Before hostilities are declared,
and before the first assault is made upon a tribe, a chal-
lenge is sent to the enemy in the form of a human hand.
The commanding officer selects some one to make the
sacrifice. The hand is held out and cut off by another
soldier. The man who takes the hand does not return
as a rule, but the hand is returned with defiance or good-
will. After a battle the soldiers are reviewed by the
king, who executes those guilty of offenses and commends
those distinguished for their bravery. On the day appointed by him to receive the chiefs the prisoners are
brought to be dealt with according to the decree of the
king. No nobleman may be reduced to slavery; he is
usually put to death. The king executes a captured king.
The following evening all engage in the glee of the war-
dance.

The members of the " Devil Bush " are not only taught
everything pertaining to practical war, but they are taught
hunting as well. They are first taught to capture small
game and later the larger and dangerous animals like the
leopard, elephant, and buffalo. What the Africans call a
real hunt requires about a month's work in preparation.
The boys dig a large pit and surround the ends and sides
with the trunks of large trees. With the pit of the apex,
in triangular form two fences are built about a mile long,
and with a mile between the two extremities. The sur-

rounding country is encircled by the hunters and the animals are driven into the pit. The smaller animals are eaten and the larger ones are sent to the king. As the valuable skins are preserved, the boys are taught to skin animals neatly. The ivories belong to the king, and various small horns are kept for amulets, and so on. These hunts are usually accompanied with much singing and dancing, after the cooking and eating of the game.

There are many other things taught in the "Devil Bush," and some of the practices to which I have referred have receded, under Liberian influence, farther into the interior, and others yet have been discontinued altogether. There is another organization called "Allebigah." This is purely a secret lodge, and has extensive influence among the Liberian tribes. The chief object of the lodge is to protect the individual member, and it is said that it will protect at all hazards. This society has lodges among the Vai, Mandingo, p esi, Buni, Bandi, Bere, Gizima, Gora, and Dé tribes.

AIM AND PRINCIPLES OF THE "GREEGREE BUSH"

The "Greegree Bush" is a society for the training of girls for future life, just as the "Devil Bush" is for boys. It is death for a man to be found within the limits of the "Greegree Bush," no matter what his purpose may be. The sessions of the society are held near some town, yet few in that town know the exact place. No one is permitted to approach the scene. It is said that the "Greegree Bush" begins when a girl who has not been in it pours water upon the head of the Zo who is generally in all the towns. Those who have been in it catch the candidate and hold her, and send word to all the neighboring towns that a " Greegree Bush " is to be organized at once. The organization is under the direction of a Zo and Zo-Nockba. The Zo is the owner of the Bush and she comes to town for the greegree plays. The Zo-Nockba is the one who is versed in the art of training the girls in the aim and principles of the Bush, and during plays remains therein. The Bush is in session from three to seven years, and may be less. Upon the death of the king or Zo the Bush always breaks up. The number of attendants may be anywhere from five to two hundred. Usually girls are admitted at seven or eight years of age, although women may be admitted. A native woman is never considered much nor is she highly respected unless she has been in this institution. At the time of entrance a little horn with medicine and some little red berries is placed on the necks of the girls. If a girl violates her virginity while this horn is on her neck, she is tied facing the violater, and they are both stripped naked and whipped publicly in the town, and must pay a large fine before they may be released. At one time the penalty was death to them both. When the Bush is over, early in the morning the Zo removes from the necks of the maids these little horns; for as long as they are worn the girls cannot marry nor must they be violated by man. They are taken to town for a " Big Play " by the Zo-ba known generally as the " Country Devil." The expense of the Bush is borne by the parents who have children there. Women are not allowed to look upon the " Country Devil." He is hideously dressed in a long gown; has a wooden head with silver stripes around the eyes, shoes on the feet, and many native additions to make his appearance as frightful as possible. I recall a visit to Dàdoo, a Vai town, where

the king had died only a few days before. The three
" Country Devils " in attendance at the plays came suddenly through the streets about 8 o'clock at night. Such
terror! The women and children,— in fact, everybody,
— were running and screaming and falling over one another in an endeavor to get into the houses. This
" Country Devil " is a woman dressed as a man. It is
impossible for anybody to see the " Country Devil " from
the " Devil Bush " unless he belongs to the society.

The " Greegree Bush " has both an industrial and an
educational purpose. The girls are taught to embroider
with gold and silver thread the tunics and togas of kings
and chiefs. Some of them become very artistic in working palm-trees, golden elephants, moons, half-moons, running vines, and other objects and scenes of nature in
various articles of apparel. The Africans have ways of
dressing hair which are peculiarly adapted to their conditions and to them. I have noticed three ways. Using
the center of the crown of the head, one way is to plait
it in rows in all directions, with the ends turned in with
a stick, comb, or ivory instrument made for the purpose.
Another way is to plait it lengthwise of the head; and
still another is to plait the hair with the ends out in single
plaits, arranged in rows. The girls are taught hair-dress-
ing in order that they may plait, besides their own, the
hair of the richer Vais, some of whom have their hair
oiled and plaited two or three times a week.

Instruction is given in cutting inscriptions on shields,
breastplates, and the like, and in housekeeping, singing,
dancing, farming, sewing, weaving cotton, dyeing, making nets and mats and many other articles of domestic
utility, decoration, and dress. I have seen Vai women
making some of the most beautiful fancy baskets of vari-

ous kinds to be found along the coast. In this institution they are also taught their duty to the king, the law, and especially that which refers to the women. The girls are taught their duty to their parents, to their future husbands, and the other duties belonging to the common lot of Vai women. Of course the influence of the " Greegree Bush " is now considerably weakened by the Liberian institutions on the one hand and the Muhammudan faith and customs on the other. So that now this institution falls far short of achieving its aims and putting into practice its principles. It has its greatest power among the people that live near the interior limits of the Vai country. Near the Liberian settlements it amounts to almost nothing.

MARRIAGE AND THE FAMILY

Courtship and marriage among the Vais seem very simple. The casual observer would think them devoid of love; but they have their romances, their loves and dreams, their Romeos and their Juliets. Behind what seem to be mere form and custom are sentiments, though crude perhaps, which in other races we call love. It is customary for the father, when he thinks necessary, to provide his sons with wives. The son may be permitted to select his own wife. In either case the preliminaries vary but little. If the girl is very small, a straw is put in her hair by the suitor or his father. When a young man sees a maid that he desires for his wife, he calls upon her parents and presents them with a present or presents, varying in value and amount according to the wealth and standing of the persons interested. This is required in order to insure good faith on the part of the suitor. The making of these presents is called a " dash," which is very popular among

VAI LEATHER SHOES AND HANDBAGS

Facing Page 56

native Africans. This " dash " may consist of gin, rum, brass kettles, cloth, and so on. At the time the suitor calls and " dashes " the parents he also confesses his love for their daughter. If the proposal is accepted and the contracting parties reside in the same town, the girl is supposed to call on the young man each day. Just as the father usually provides his sons with wives, so the parents of the girls generally arrange for their husbands.

The majority of the girls are placed in the " Greegree Bush," and when they come out, if they are not already betrothed, they are in the marriage market. Very few girls in families of standing are not engaged long before they enter the " Greegree Bush." I have been informed that they have been pledged in instances before they were born, of course on the condition that they should prove to be girls. The explanation of this is family prestige. When a girl is about to be married she must be washed. The washing is supposed to wash away the " Greegree Bush Devil." For as long as she is unwashed she cannot be married. There is some expense connected with this washing, which is borne by the parents of the bride-to-be. When the man has built his home and is ready for his wife, her people dress her up and take her to him. The groom then " dashes " her entire family,— giving them leopard teeth, kettles, cloth, and one or two servants, the amount never being less than the expenditures of the parents in the rearing of the girl, including her training in the " Greegree Bush." During the period of engagement the young man must present from time to time to the parents of his betrothed gifts of such things as they may need and desire.

When a young man marries a girl from another town, she brings to her husband some of everything she has, such as rice, plettoes, wori, salt, pepper, honey, palm oil, water, and even small fish, which she throws into the streams. She does this for independence,— so that if at any time she is taunted by her new acquaintances of the town, she may reply that she has brought her own things, and is therefore independent of them. Virginity is very highly prized by the Vais, as it is among most African tribes unaffected by outside influences. It is the custom of the parents to guarantee the virtue of their daughter given in marriage. Some member of the groom's family is selected to remain concealed near the room of the newly married couple for a few days after the marriage in order to secure the evidence of the bride's virginity. If she is not a virgin, the husband may annul the marriage if he so desires. He may recover what he has spent in "dashes" to the girl and her parents in his suit. On the other hand, if she proves to be a virgin, the husband shoots a gun. He breaks the good news to his wife's family and accompanies it with presents. And for two or three days there is a general rejoicing in both families and among their friends.

The family among the Vais is polygamous. This form of marriage naturally leads to a broader definition of that term than the one that is accepted among the civilized nations of to-day. All the relatives of a Vai man and his wife are members of his family. Every man may have one or more wives, but he must provide a separate house for each one. While every man may have plural wives, there are some who have but one. But those who practise monogamy are not so many, I think, as has been supposed by some people who have given attention to native Africans. I am led to this conclusion by the fact that the poor men are about as able to buy the poor women as

the richer men are to buy the richer women. Moreover,
the Vai women, when once obtained, are a source of
economic strength to the family. By their industry most
of the farming is carried on, and most of the products for
dress and domestic use are made by their skill. Also the
women obtain and prepare most of the articles for domestic and foreign trade.

The Vai women generally are gentle to their children,
and sometimes very loving. The rights of parents over
their issue have been very great. At one time children
might be killed for disobedience and disrespect, but Liberian and other influences wrought some modifications.
A child may still be pawned. Along the coast the marriage bond is very loose, but far into the interior a wife
may not be put aside at the pleasure of her husband.
When men are away for a time, upon their return they
test the fidelity of their wives by the sassawood ordeal.[1]
This ordeal is very much dreaded, and no doubt is a very
strong deterrent to some women who might be tempted
to be unfaithful. When a wife leaves her husband for
another man, the husband may recover from the latter, in
addition to the purchase money, the value of every article
that he has given to his wife during their marriage. If
she leaves for any other reason, the husband may compel
her return through her parents or the return of the purchase money and the value of all gifts that have been
made to the daughter.

A wife may be divorced for witchcraft or adultery, but
for the latter a valuable consideration in goods and money
is often accepted by the injured husband. When a Vai
man has a number of wives he always has a head wife to
whom the other wives are somewhat subordinate; and

[1] See Chapter V, 3, Oaths, Ordeals, etc.

upon his death his wives become the property of his eldest brother.[2]   And the head wife does not become the property of the eldest son, as Mr. Ellis observed was the case among the Yoruba-Speaking Peoples of the Slave Coast of West Africa.[3]

THE SCOPE AND INFLUENCE OF WITCHCRAFT

Witchcraft is common to certain stages of intellectual growth.

"It is shaken off," says Mr. Draper, "as men and nations approach maturity."[4]

We readily understand how natural it is for "childhood to people solitude and darkness with unrealities"; we ought as readily to comprehend how men and nations, in intellectual infancy, inhabit the universe with creatures of their fancy, and how they must in time throw those creatures aside as naturally as the developed mind dispels the delusions of earlier years.   Every great nation of the earth has had its beliefs in some form of witchcraft.   In early times some of these forms existed among the Arabians; later they were found among the Hebrews, Greeks, and Romans,[5] and finally they held sway among the modern nations of Europe.   Shakespeare opens Macbeth with the conversation between three witches, and in Act IV, Scene 3, speaks of the crew of wretched souls which stay the cure of maladies, and describes how the king by a simple touch cures people swollen and ulcerous,

[2] But they may marry other relatives.
[3] "The Yoruba-Speaking Peoples," p. 185.
[4] "Intellectual Development of Europe," by J. W. Draper, p. 119.
[5] "Intellectual Development of Europe," by J. W. Draper, Vol. II, pp. 116-117.

" pitiful to the eye, the mere despair of surgery."

It is said that Dr. Johnson when a boy was touched by Queen Anne, and Mr. Draper quotes a passage which shows that so eminent a reformer as Luther was not entirely free from the baneful influence of witchcraft. History records that witches were put to death in Massachusetts; and Mr. Lecky reminds us that the belief in the king's touch as a cure for scrofula was asserted by the clergy in the palmiest days of the English Church by the great University of Oxford, and survived the ages of the Reformation, of Bacon and Milton, and Hobbes and Locke.[6] You will hardly read a more eloquent description of the physical phenomena which combined to produce the witch of Scotland than those impressive lines of Buckle, in which he portrays the character of this mistress of the Scottish demons, arisen from the decrepit hag of England to the mastery of evil spirits, spreading among the people the desolation and despair of terror.[7]

It is natural, therefore, that we should expect to find some strange superstitions among the Vais, surrounded as they are by the peculiar and extraordinary conditions of West Africa. We are not to be disappointed, for they believe that their dead are transformed into animals and birds and return to certain persons who employ them to the injury of others. The varied and unexplained phenomena of nature have impressed the Vai men with the existence of countless invisible spirits which visit calamity and death upon them. They believe that these spirits are in league with or under the direction of certain people,

[6] "History of European Morals," by W. E. H. Lecky, Vol. I, pp. 363-364.
[7] "Introduction to the History of Civilization in England," by H. Thomas Buckle, p. 649, revised by John M. Robertson.

commonly known as wizards and witches, whom they call sua-kai and sua-musu. A person practising witchery is called a sua-mo,— sua meaning milt, which is used to test the practice of witchcraft, and mo meaning man, or person.

If anybody dies suddenly and mysteriously, it is believed that he is either a witch or has been witched. A post mortem examination is held.[8] If certain portions inside are found black and the sua refuses to float, the person is pronounced a witch. If he be a man, he is a sua-kai; if a woman, a sua-musu. The body is dishonored, deprived of all death ceremonies, and is hurried outside the limits of the town. This disgrace is supposed to attach to the family of the discovered witch.

In case the test fails to establish the person as a witch, they set about to find the witch who caused the death of the deceased. In order to prove guilt or innocence, a number of suspected persons are subjected to one of the native ordeals.[9] Somebody is usually convicted and suffers the death and disgrace of a witch. This is the most dreaded and dangerous class of witches. It is believed that they go about at night riding people and bringing upon them sickness, death, and all kinds of calamities.

The Vais have among them a man whom they call a beri-mo,— beri meaning medicine, greegree, or poison, and mo meaning man. He is commonly called a medicine-man. This was no doubt his original vocation, as indicated by the name,— to administer medicine to the sick. But he has undergone an evolution and has considerably increased his functions. He has been instrumental in spreading the belief that he is in communion

[8] Everybody is examined after they are dead except Muhammudans and the chief women of the " Greegree Bush."
[9] Chapter V, 3.

with the invisible spirits and exercises some control over their conduct, so that the Vais believe that they can secure medicine from the beri-mo that will bring evil upon an enemy. His services are secured to witch an adversary, and the last of his many added powers is to give medicine that will counteract the influence of witch-medicine prepared by another beri-mo.

There is a belief, as I have stated, among the Vais that witches come to your house and ride you at night,— that when the witch comes in the door he takes off his skin and lays it aside in the house. It is believed that he returns you to the bed where he found you, and that the witch may be killed by sprinkling salt and pepper in certain portions of the room, which will prevent the witch from putting on his skin.' Just before they go to bed it is a common thing to see Vai people sprinkling salt and pepper about the room.

It is also believed that witches take babies out at night and sacrifice them at witch-plays. It is believed that the babies are cooked in the small country pots. Parents often go to the beri-mo and get medicine which is put in a horn and placed on the outside of the door of the suspected witch; that is sufficient to keep the witch from entering the house and getting into his skin, which may be seen in the bed. They say the horn will fight the witch at the door until daylight, when they can catch the witch. The person suspected is actually in the house in bed, but they say that is only his skin, and cite instances when by this method they have caught witches.

The alligator is sacred to the Vais. Along the rivers and the banks of the Peso Lake they are frequent visitors of the native towns. To kill one, they say, is death. Among the Vais there are alligator societies, the objects of which are to enrich the members and make them able through witchcraft to destroy their enemies.   It requires the strongest nerve to become a member of one of these societies, for if required to do so one must sacrifice the dearest of his relatives.   In order to join one must pay the required fee and " dash " to a member who goes to consult the alligators.   He returns and generally reports the sacrifice to be made of a mother, father, or child, according to the designation of the alligators.   If the person consents to the sacrifice, his application is accepted, and he is cautioned to be brave-hearted and to fear nothing he may see or hear.   If the candidate is willing to continue, on a night and place selected by the alligators, usually some river or lake, the applicant is led by the alligator-medicine-man into the water until it extends above his waist.   The medicine-man again cautions him about being afraid of sights or sounds.   He tells the candidate he will hear awful sounds and see four monstrous alligators, but he must not fear; that he must put his hand into the mouth of the fourth one, and take out the leaves to be found there.   His hand must not tremble, lest it should get injured against the alligator's teeth.   Then the medicine-man disappears.

While the applicant is waiting alone the waters become disturbed, he hears a frightful noise, and three alligators approach, with a most vicious and menacing grin.   He stands unmoved.   Another frightful noise is heard, and a fourth alligator swims up, with open mouth.   He calmly takes out the leaves, after which the medicine-man returns, and instructs him how to use them when he wishes to call the alligator and communicate to it his wishes.   He then buys an alligator for himself alone,— an alligator that is to come at his call.   It is said that many people become so enraptured with their alligators that the death of the latter means the death of the former. The natives appear to be sincere when they give instances where persons have immediately died after the death of their alligators. Some of these instances may be explained by mere coincidence, the others, I think, by suicide,— that is, the owner chooses death after having been deprived of his alligator and poisons himself.

During the early settlement of Cape Mount, the alligators were very troublesome to the Liberians, and they often destroyed children along the river. I am informed that a native boy passed through the yard of a Liberian woman, who asked him to bring her a pail of water from a brook near by, and offered the boy a small " dash." The boy refused and made some unpleasant answer, whereupon the woman said,

" Go on; the alligators will soon eat you."

And in less than ten minutes a loud noise called the woman to the door, only to see a stream of blood and the mangled body of the little boy. As she hastened to the door little did she think and expect to see that her thoughtless prediction had come true. A native man who was standing near when she had announced this cruel fate said to the woman in his broken English,

" Mammy, be you up country, we burn you for witch."

At that moment they heard the reports of guns and saw people coming in from all directions to see the alligator which had caused so much destruction. Among those who came was a native man, who arrived just in time to say:

" Too late; you have killed my medicine and killed myself."

It is said he died shortly afterward.

The people who deal with alligators say they have certain times to see the alligators at their houses. When the time arrives the husband instructs his wives to remain away from the house and allow no one to approach. The Vais believe that the alligators turn to beautiful maidens, and that at their homes they spend hours in the art of witchcraft. It is said that the alligator brings money in his mouth whenever it is requested to do so.

The Vais consider the owl the king of all witches. They believe that some old king transformed himself into the owl and became the king of witchcraft. The owl is called húhu. Whenever the cry of this bird is heard they tremble with fear. It is said when an owl sits upon a home at least one of its inmates is sure to die.

SOCIAL FUNCTIONS, DEATHS, AND DANCES

Among the Vais nearly all the ceremonies have a social phase; therefore, to this extent they are social functions. So that without a careful inquiry into the aim of these ceremonies and what constitutes their distinguishing feature it is very easy to conclude that they are all alike. It has seemed to me that the various ceremonies of the Vais naturally divide themselves into two classes,— one with social enjoyment as the dominant note, and the other in which the spirit of sacrifice prevails. It is the former we are to consider.

Unlike the Yoruba and Ewe-Speaking Peoples, the Vais have no ceremonies at the birth of children. In this respect they differ from some of the tribes in Liberia. When a Vai child is born, after a few days some of the

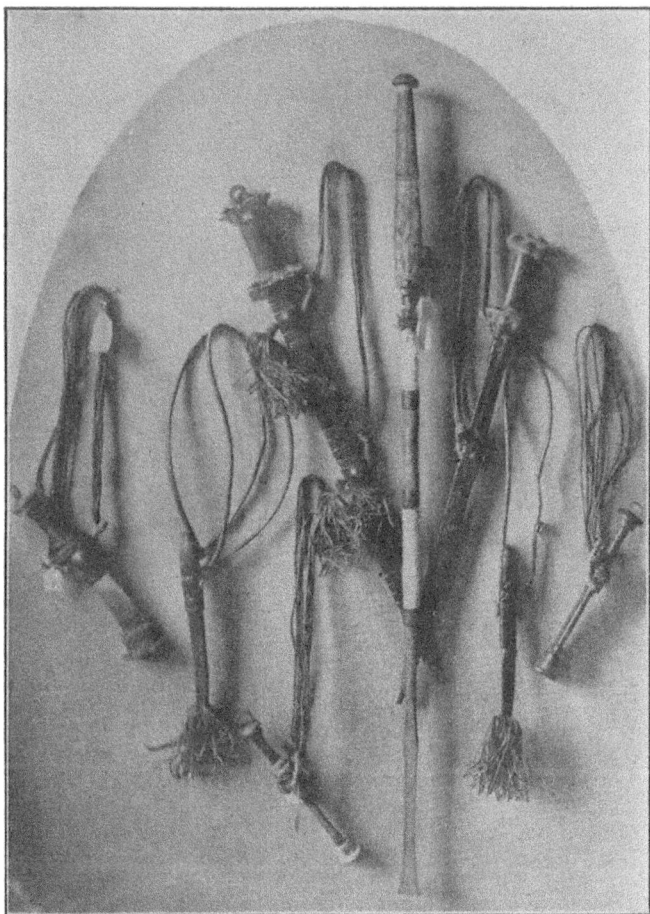

VAI SPEAR AND KNIVES IN LEATHER

Facing Page 66

elder relatives take it from the room of its birth and name it for some member of the family, or for an ancestor or an insect or an animal, or some object in nature. The name of the child depends almost entirely upon the impression made by its birth, appearance, or conduct. The name of the inventor of the Vai language is Búkere, — bu meaning gun, and kere war. The two words together mean gun-war, and was no doubt suggested by a war in which guns were used. Búkere himself gave this interpretation to the Rev. Koelle.[10] I know Vai men with the following names: Kari, serpent; Wonye, ant; Vombe, rat; Wuro, baboon; Tuna, flying dog; Tia, chicken; Surisuri, mosquito; and many others might be given in illustration of this practice.

The first name given is the surname. When the child is placed in the " Greegree Bush " or " Devil Bush "[11] it receives an additional name something like our Christian name, and upon the profession of Muhammudanism another is added, the last being always placed first. This is the key to the understanding of the Vai names. Many are to be found like the name of the Vai inventor, Momoru Doalu Búkere. When a person has only two names the supposition is either that he has not entered the beri or that he has not accepted Muhammudanism. Momoru, the Vai for Muhammud, is a very common name among the Vais.

Perhaps the first social ceremony in the life of the individual is experienced on entering the beri and sande institutions. The boys receive on their backs the national mark [12] and their second name, and they are circumcised

[10] Vai Grammar, by the Rev. S. W. Koelle, p. 19.
[11] " Devil Bush " in Vai, beri; " Greegree Bush " in Vai, sande.
[12] See Chapter II, 3, " Decoration and Dress."

if they have not been when quite small, according to custom. The above ceremony is known as the beri-rite, in connection with which is prepared a large feast called the gbána. Very often the dishes for this feast are prepared in town and not in the beri, as was formerly done, so that you will now more often hear this feast called the gbána-bo. Bo is a verb meaning to bring out, and it is added to indicate the change in the place where the food is prepared. In both the beri and sande institutions there is a cleaned place in the forest known as fari, in which all the beri and sande ceremonies are held. After the beri-rite and feast a great dance is held in the fari, aecompanied by singing and the beating of drums.

The head of the sande is called Zo-sande, and of the beri, Zo-beri. When these institutions come to a close, for weeks the beri-moenu [13] are the occasions of many social gatherings. The first one is given when the Zo-ba brings them to the nearest town. All who have finished the beri and sande rites are held in the highest esteem, and many functions are given in their honor. They are dressed in the best attire [14] their people can afford, and they march through the streets of the town as if each one were walking for a prize. This is the great Vai commencement. To witness this brilliant and grand display people come in from all the neighboring towns. Parents gather with their friends to see the evidences of what their children have learned. The zest of hope brings the lover to see his maid. Some come to eat, drink, and be merry, and others to judge the utility and efficiency of the greatest institutions of the Vais. There is a large and sump-

[13] Beri-moeuu, the plural of beri-mo, which means one who has gone through the beri-rite.
[14] See Chapter II, 3, "Decoration and Dress."

tuons feast of chickens, goats, bullocks, and African products. After the dinner the dancing begins, and late at night one can hear the singing and the dull sound of drums keeping time for those still held by the charms of the dance. When this "Big Play" is over the beri-mocuu go to their home towns, and there they are received with great rejoicing and social functions, with the native concomitants of eating and dancing.

Before those who have had the beri and sande rites can marry they must go through a ceremony commonly known as "Washing from the Devil and Greegree Bushes." Certain instructions are given in these institutions regarding the sexes, and it is believed that if they are violated by those trained in them, the violations will be attended by severe punishments. So in washing it is believed that the force and effect of the instructions are removed. After the washing a dinner is prepared, after which comes the dance with its music and singing. The washing and dinner are attended by the friends of the family, whose entertainment and pleasure make up the social feature of the ceremony.

Whenever a death occurs among the important men and women of the tribe it is always followed by a "Big Play." And for more than a week relatives and friends come with presents to the bereaved family. The women shave their heads and weep in sackcloth and ashes, assisted by professional mourners. In the event that relatives required for the final burial are absent, a temporary grave is made in the house, usually in the kitchen, for from two weeks to a year. When all the persons required have arrived, the body of the deceased is buried before the house, generally in the yard. A large feast is spread. The maids dress and march through the streets. The singers sing, and the drums announce the merriment of the day. It is a social function in which everybody is supposed to participate. They dance until a late hour at night. From appearances no one would think that a funeral ceremony was still being performed.[15]

I learned that this strange custom is founded on the belief that the dead are where they can behold the conduct of the living. The latter believe if they do not honor the dead with a " Big Play " as they honor the living the dead will be displeased and visit upon them sickness, death, and other calamities. The extent of the feast and play varies with the wealth and distinction of the family of the dead. The male relatives of the deceased as a mark of mourning wear a bana, a small ring of bamboo bark, round their heads while the females wear it about their necks. The death of a man of high standing generally leaves a number of widows. If a male relative of the deceased desires to marry one he may propose by sending her what they call a fara sunda, a bamboo-band. If she accepts the proposal, she keeps the band ; if she declines, she returns it.

Doubtless the most distinguished gathering among the native Africans is at the coronation of their king. Many Vai men of importance and letters have tried to tell me of the magnificence of the occasions when in the past the Vais have crowned their real kings. From them all I gather that it was the custom for the king to be attired in robes of scarlet or some brilliant color, adorned with tiger skins and made especially for the occasion. By the most skilful of native hands his robes had been figured with the forms of various animals. He wore the rarest

[15] I was at the town of Bomie when the Vai king died, on April 28, 1904, in the Vai country.

designs of the most expensive native jewelry made of gold and silver. His carved breastplate hung on his neck, and on his wrists were a number of leopard teeth. On his head he wore a cap, or king's hat, ornamented with shells and the fur of animals. Attended by all his chiefs and warriors, he appeared for the coronation. The head medicine-man sprinkles the king with powder and greases his face with oil and ointments. The king kneels before the medicine-man. Volleys of shot are fired by the soldiers near by, and in a little while he is declared king. The king is given a reception. A general dance is commenced, forming a circle about him; the music starts, the drums and clappers sound, and the dance continues. In order to express his admiration now and then a dancer or musician prostrates himself at the king's feet. And the ceremony is concluded for a while by serving him rum, wine, and whiskey. The king retires until the feast is announced. He again joins his subjects in partaking of the various native dishes, after which he is ready for the final act of the ceremony. The king is seated on his stool or chair, ready for the sacrifice, when the poor victims are brought forward and executed.

A sham battle follows, in which the generals and warriors of the realm vie with one another in the exhibition of their military tactics and skill. From all the towns come the best singers, clappers, drummers, and other musicians, to make the music for a grand dance in the square,[16] which is usually in the center of the town. The Zo-bas or " Country Devils " lead the way for the best dancers of the country. From the circle to the square from 1 to 300

[16] It is not really a square; it is an open place left for public functions and the dance, near the centre of the town; sometimes it is square, and sometimes it is not.

women, trained in the art of the native dance, make many figures, and some of them are so zealous and fantastic in their movements that they are borne exhausted from the dance.

It is hardly necessary to mention the dance as a social function. It is one of the principal features of all native gatherings of whatever nature. In all the ceremonies of the beri and sande institutions,— such as the naming of children, marriages and deaths, and the functions in honor of the king,— the dance ranks with the feast. And these two together constitute the essence of all social expression among the Vais. It is a common saying that "When the sun goes down all Africa dances." [17] During suitable weather in almost every town there is a dance every evening.

But there are various kinds of dances. Besides the common dance, the timbo, there is the ziawa, a dance accompanied by a peculiar kind of song; the ngere, another dance with a special song, and the mazu, a dance accompanied by wild gestures of the arms. In the beri and sande societies special instruction is given in dancing, and many Vai women are graceful as well as highly proficient in the native art. On lovely evenings the professional singers and dancers go from house to house, singing and dancing for the rich, for which they receive the customary "dashes."

[17] This often made statement is hardly true. Those who dance do so a great deal, but the great majority of Africans dance very little if any more than other races. Especially is this true of the Islamic tribes.

CHAPTER V

POLITICS AND GOVERNMENT OF THE VAIS

NATURE AND FORM OF GOVERNMENT

IN nature and form the Government of the Vais is monarchial. The Vai country is situated in the British Colony of Sierra Leone and the Republic of Liberia, but principally in the latter. The whole is divided into petty kingdoms: Garwoola, Tombei, Teywa, Konae, Sowolo, and Jaryalor, the last two of which are known as Gallinas and are in the colony of Sierra Leone. The general laws are made by the kings of the different sections of the Vai territory in joint session, and by them communicated to their respective peoples. The Vais near Cape Mount elected a king April 25, 1904. A few days later I visited near the scene in a trip across the Vai country. A Vai man by the name of Gonda was made king. For this kingship for more than a century there have been two rival families,—the Bessy and Sandfish houses. The contests waged by the factions attached to these royal families have been the source of much trouble and bloodshed among the Vai people.

Although Gonda was elected king of a section of the Vais, the governments of the sections have always been hereditary monarchies.[1] The king, or koro-mandsa, is

[1] At Cape Mount the Vais over whom Gonda was elected king were called the Màfà people by the Americo-Liberians with whom I conversed, and those on the lake the Peso, for the lake.

the supreme head. The will of the king is limited by a supreme council composed of the noblemen of the realm, and by a kind of unwritten constitution, founded in the necessities for social life and intercourse. This unwritten constitution contains the understood natural rights of free Vai men, recognized and sanctioned by the practice of generations. The throne descends to the eldest son, if he be of age. No minor can become king. If there be no direct male heir capable of assuming the reins of government, it falls to the eldest brother of the king; if there be no eligible brother, then to the eldest nephew. No female can occupy the throne, according to customary law. Yet a woman has ruled over a portion of the Vai country.

Taradoba was the favorite wife of King Arma, who died from a wound received in battle.[2] The Capitol of his kingdom was at Bendoo. King Arma had a very ambitious brother who was king over a large number of people northwest of the Vai country, and upon the death of the former he usurped his throne and made himself king over the Vais. Taradoba with five or six hundred warriors of her dead husband took possession of a southern province. By the new king of the Vais three attempts were made to subdue her, but she successfully repelled each invasion. It is said that she commanded her troops in person, distinguishing herself with such valor and success that one might fittingly refer to her as the Jeanne d'Arc of the Vais. She ruled for many years, and her son, Momolu Massaquoi, educated at Central Tennessee College, is now king over the Gallinas.[3]

[2] Taradoba is generally known by the name Sandemande. Taradoba is a Gora word meaning brave, and it was given to Sandemande on account of her prowess. King Arma died 25 or 30 years ago.

[3] His right is now, however, being contested by Sandemanna, a

VAI HOES, PIPE, SNUFF HORN, WHIP, &c.

Facing Page

As far as I have been able to ascertain there is no definite tax levied by the king upon the people. It is a law that when any large meat is killed, like an elephant or a leopard, it belongs to the king. He always takes the head containing the teeth and the tusks which are very valuable, the former as articles of native dress, the latter principally as articles for export. It is also customary when the chiefs and important men from the provinces call upon the king to bring " dashes," consisting of rice, palm oil, servants, cloth, and so on. Besides, the king and members of his council receive compensation in settling disputes arising between the subjects. He also has a large number of domestic and field servants who produce whatever is desired. The other members of the council also receive " dashes " and have servants for the farm and trade.

DISTRIBUTION OF POLITICAL POWER

Among infant peoples governments derive their ultimate sanctions from force. The supreme power of the king is in his army. All the civil and political institutions receive added strength from the prestige of the king that is acquired in arms. So far as I have been able to observe the power of government among the Vais as yet has not been definitely differentiated into well established and co-ordinate branches, with separate administrative officers supreme in their spheres. The departments of government are somewhat confused and very often have common officers. The king has his trusted generals, and the chiefs of provinces and towns usually command their men in war. The same chiefs are also the principal officers in

Vai prince educated in England. He is now Chief Clerk in the Liberian Department of State at Monrovia, Liberia, the legislative, judicial, and executive government of the towns and half-towns and make up the supreme council of the state. The officer next in rank to the king is the prime-minister, called bore-be-den. The Vai word for chief of a town is mandas.

In the government of the kingdom all matters, whether military or civil, affecting the tribe or disputes arising between subjects of different provinces are decided by the king, prime minister, and the chiefs of the provinces who make up the council to the king. All matters affecting a province or town are decided by the chief of the province, with the chiefs of the towns as his council; and in case of a town, by the chief thereof and the elders of the town as council. In half-towns the sub-chiefs have jurisdiction over matters therein, and may call other sub-chiefs to sit in the cases with them. The chief of a province may also call to sit with him chiefs of other provinces. The king is chief of the province and town in which he lives. The prime minister is usually chief of a province or of a town or of both. One may appeal from the sub-chief to the chief of a town, thence to the chief of a province, and finally to the king.

FORMS OF OATHS AND ORDEALS

Among the Vais are various forms of oaths. Among them I might mention the cassava-oath, the war-oath, and the medicine-oath. These oaths are used on different occasions, yet the binding force and effect of each is substantially the same. The oaths taken by the Vais and other Africans in this part of West Africa are much more serious than oaths taken in civilized lands. Each oath-taker affirms that if he breaks his oath he should die or must die in a certain manner by definite means, and if he breaks it he usually dies in the manner indicated.   The medicine-oath is usually employed in ordinary matters where one swears to tell the truth.   The medicine is wrapped in a piece of flannel and placed on a plate on which the oath-taker knocks with a small stick as he takes the oath.

The war-oath is taken by the soldiers, binding themselves to the king before going to war.   The soldier taking this oath, while taking it, has a sword held to his throat as he beats with a small stick on a vessel containing medicine prepared by the native doctor.   The sword is used in this oath because by it the soldier usually meets his death.   The warrior is very skilful with the sword, and can cut off a man's head with a single stroke.   To break this war-oath is to insure certain death.   The cassava-oath may also be used in civil matters, but when taken in connection with the spear it is very often employed in making terms of peace between warring tribes.

In August, 1904, a convocation of native kings was called at Monrovia, Liberia, to settle the intertribal war of the interior.   There were in attendance about eighteen kings with twelve or fifteen hundred attendants.   At the conclusion of the conference the kings took the cassava-oath.   When this oath is about to be administered a gun is fired within the hearing of all.   This means that if the oath be broken the next gunshot heard afterwards by the perjurer is to sound his death.   The gun is washed out with water, which is preserved in a large bowl.   In this black water are dissolved salt, powder, and ashes, and into this concoction are placed small pieces of cassava.   Near by are bottles of gin.   And when a spear is stuck into the ground with the point upwards everything is ready for the taking of the oath.   Every native man is

supposed to use these articles, some of them at least,—
salt, powder, and cassava. The taking of these neces-
saries signifies that if the oath-breaker has any of them
in his stomach or eats any of them thereafter, they will
help to kill him. The ashes are used to scour out the
stomach and are supposed to assist the other articles in
punishing the perjurer.

Some disinterested person hands some of the medicine
in a spoon from the bowl to the oath-taker after he has
taken a piece of cassava with his mouth from the spear.
As he eats the cassava the person or persons with whom he
has had difficulty states the elements of the oath he must
take. The person being sworn accompanies his eating
cassava with frequent draughts of gin as he repeats the
oath and concludes with the hope that if he breaks his
oath his country will grow up in bush and that the medicine will kill him. In order to aid the action and to
increase the effect of the medicine the stomach is given
a thorough cleaning out the day before the oath is to be
taken.

So much importance was attached to the oaths of Kings
Pomopora and Tavadadua that I will venture to give them
as recorded in my stenographic report of the proceedings
of the conference. The following is the oath of Tavadadua:

" That if he brings war upon Pomopora, the medicine must kill him; that if there is any breaking of the
oaths and he refuses to call Pomopora to the Government, the medicine must kill him; that if any war is made
north of the St. Paul River before it is returned it must
be brought to the Government at Monrovia, and if he
fails to do this the medicine must kill him."

In taking this oath King Tavadadua drank the medicine after he had taken the cassava from the spear with his mouth. He held in his hand a small stick, which he beat on the bowl as he repeated his oath. The same was done by Pomopora, whose oath is as follows:

" That he had heard of war, but if he had sent war to Gorgie the medicine must kill him; that if any further war is started and he goes and joins it, the medicine must kill him; that if he hears any war news and fails to report it to the Government, the medicine must kill him."

At this point Tavadadua had the following incorporated in Pomopora's oath:

" That if Pomopora hears of any war from the p esi or Bele country against Tavadadua, he must report the same to the Government, and if he does not do so, the medicine must kill him."

After the above oaths were taken they both joined in this oath:

" That if they go into any war or hire anybody to fight the other or any of his people, the medicine must kill them,"

and they further swear

" that if either of them hire anybody to give poison to any of the other's people or to either of them, the medicine must kill him." [4]

Like the oaths, the ordeals are many in form but one

[4] Taken as given by an interpreter, a native chief who spoke 8 or 10 different tribal languages.

in purpose and effect. They are all devices in the hands of the medicine-man by means of which the people seek to detect crime and to ascertain the infidelity of wives. The ordeals of the country bowl and mortar pestle are about the same and are frequently used in cases of stealing. When anything has been stolen, for instance, a number of suspects are stood in a row. The medicine-man prepares his medicine, and while he is mumbling some unintelligible words some one passes with the bowl or mortar along the line of suspects, and the bowl or pestle is supposed to knock against the guilty person. The person toward whom is directed the greatest suspicion is generally the person knocked by the bowl or mortar. Everything depends upon the medicine-man, who is governed generally by public sentiment but is not proof against influence and bribes.

There is an ordeal of hot iron used both in the cases of stealing and of the infidelity of a wife as well as to prove innocence in general. A person charged with a crime must be willing to undergo the iron test or be considered guilty. When he stands the test the medicine-man washes out the mouth of the accused with his medicine and then inserts a red-hot iron. If he is innocent, it is believed that the iron will not burn the mouth of the person charged. It is the common belief that few if any guilty persons stand the test, so that most of the persons who stand it are innocent. It is said by some that the medicine-man washes out the mouth with a certain kind of medicine which prevents the iron from burning when he so desires, and vice versa. Many innocent people who are unable to satisfy the medicine-man get burned and are condemned. And it is thought that some guilty people may escape by buying the favor of the medicine-man.

The ordeal of placing the hand in boiling-hot palm oil is used also when the wife is charged with being unfaithful, or when any person is charged with a crime. To prove innocence one must submit to the test. It is believed that the hand is protected by certain medicine with which it is washed in the case of hot palm oil, as the mouth is in the case of the hot iron, and this ceremony, too, takes place under the same conditions and influences. To test the fidelity of the wife many ordeals are resorted to, but the favorite one is to make her drink sassawood tea. This ordeal is also used to prove innocence. In either case the person is supposed to drink about one quart of sassawood tea, which is rank poison. If the sassawood is immediately thrown up the person is innocent; if not, he is guilty and must suffer according to his offense. It is thought that the medicine-man makes this tea weak or strong to suit his plan to acquit or condemn,— that is, that the sassawood tea made a certain strength will be thrown up, and if not so made will be retained.

In all the ordeals the medicine-man takes good pains to get his fee in advance. I remember another ordeal employed by a Vai doctor to prove the guilt of a man who was said to have stolen a watch in Monrovia some time in August, 1904. A European had just arrived in town. He went to his apartments, took off his coat and vest, and laid them on the bed. In his vest he had a valuable gold watch, which was almost immediately stolen therefrom by one of the several native men employed about the house. In the town was a Vai medicine-man who claimed he could find out the thief. He took charge of the case, and had all the men in the house brought before him. He prepared his medicine, took three sheets of paper, wrote in his book, and while asking questions had each suspect draw the papers from the book three times. He said that on the third drawing, if the person were guilty, the paper would turn red. I was informed that the test was tried twice and that each time the same man was convicted.

There were some who doubted the correctness of the tests, and the Vai doctor tried another with the same result. He took a small rough stone and placed it three times under the lid of the eye of each person suspected. He said that the third time the stone would pass under the eyelid of the guilty party, and could be felt beneath the skin of the head. I was informed by many who saw the ordeal that the stone dropped each time from the eye of all but one man,— the one already convicted by the test of the papers turning red,— and that the third time it was put under the eyelid of this man it actually went up into his head. They said that one could see the upraised skin on his head made by the stone, that the man suffered great agony, and that to save his life the doctor had to remove the stone. This medicine-man was a very clever man, for I know he secured by his ordeals the faith and confidence of some rather intelligent men. I had this doctor call on me, but he soon discovered my object and I could not get him to perform anything before me or to call again.[5]

CRIMES AND THE ADMINISTRATION OF JUSTICE

The administration of justice among the Vais is very simple. The cases arising from time to time are divided into two classes,— criminal and civil. In each town and half-town there is a court, of which the chief or sub-chief

[5] I recall a form of oath very sacred, taken by kings in times of mutual danger, to bind themselves together. It consists in touching the ground, pointing toward the sky, then touching the tongue with the finger employed in the action.

is judge. From what I have been able to learn crimes have almost the same status as civil cases; that is to say, the state does not recognize offenses as crimes against the state or society except in the cases of capital offenses. The injured family may or may not invoke the power of the Government. It may compromise a crime with the offending family, or person, as in a civil case, but when once the Government is appealed to its judgments are executed with strictness according to the native law.

Murder, treason, and witchcraft are punishable by death. Such crimes as rape,[6] abduction, seduction, adultery, arson, and theft are punished by fines, imprisonment, or flogging. The tendency,— and the more common practice,— is to compel offenders to pay costs and a certain amount in goods to the injured party as in civil cases. In criminal matters appeals may be taken up as in civil matters. The practice is general among the Vais in criminal cases to appeal to some one or more of the ordeals and to abide the result. The authority of the state is invoked only when some satisfactory settlement cannot be made privately.

When a criminal or civil case reaches the court, the procedure is the same. In either case the law among the Vais, as among most peoples, is expensive. A person desiring to enter a suit calls upon the chief of a town and presents him with a "dash" called "cold water,"— a much appreciated article in tropical Africa. This "dash" may consist of rum, gin, tobacco, and so on. After the "dash" the chief hears the statement of the case. When it is finished he sends his messenger with

[6] Rape is a capital offense when committed against sande girls and members of prominent families.

his cane or whip [7] and summons his assistant and the elders of the town.   He summons the defendant, and next the medicine-man to administer the oaths to the witnesses in the case.   After the taking of the oaths the testimony begins.   During the hearing of the testimony the members of the court ask such questions as they desire.

When the testimony is finished both the plaintiff and defendant must " dash " the court; they call this " dash " putting them in the path.   Every member of the court except the chief votes, and a majority rules.   When the case is a tie each side pays half of the cost.   In coming from the consultation the court is not allowed to talk to anybody.   Before the members of the court can sit down after they have returned they must have another " dash " of cloth, gin, tobacco, and so on.   In delivering the judgment the assistant chief speaks for the chief.   Before the assistant talks they must be " dashed " again so the palaver,[8] as they say, can be talked easy.   If the plaintiff wins the case the judgment is that the defendant shall pay all costs, pay the amount adjudged to be due the plaintiff, and in addition give him one gown to put the said plaintiff in the path.   It is believed that the plaintiff would have difficulty in finding the path home unless he should be given this gown.[9]

[7] The king or chief has a symbol of authority which he carries and which he gives his messenger when he summons anyone. When the subjects see this symbol they dare not disobey the summons.

[8] An adopted word used by the natives to express trouble or difficulty in any form and under any conditions.

[9] Vais believe every man is in the right path, hence the requirement when he is disturbed or taken out that he be put back.

CHAPTER VI

RELIGIOUS LIFE AND PRACTICE OF THE VAIS

IDEA AND CONCEPTION OF GOD

THE religious life and practice of the Vais consist of two elements,— the pagan and the Muhammudan. The former is their own. With all its defects, superstitions, and mysteries, it is still the means by which they have sought to find and serve their God. In a private conversation Dr. Blyden once said to me that " every race must find God for itself." Then the pagan life of the Vais is interesting to students of native religions in Africa. The religion of the Vais is a form of pantheism, and can best be understood from the religious acts of the people. They conceive God as the controller of the earth and skies and as manifesting Himself in spirits and natural phenomena. They think He is too far away to serve them Himself, and that therefore it is not necessary to worship Him directly.[1] This is a natural conception, for the ruling classes of Africans are accustomed to send their servants or slaves to attend to their affairs. When the people suffer any calamity they believe that their God is displeased with them, and that in some specific way an evil spirit has been chosen to punish them. Hence one finds the Vais wearing amulets sacred to their God and believ-

[1] This is not true of the Africans who have embraced the faith of Muhammud.

85

ing in the efficacy of these charms as long as they are worn.   One will see them making sacrifices to natural things, not as if to God but as if to an object through which a spirit acted to their detriment or in which it dwells, and against whose displeasure it is necessary to protect themselves.

So that the religious life of the pagan Vais is associated with certain natural objects or phenomena which are believed to have rendered service, conferred favors, or inflicted injury upon the people, and which are thought to be the abodes of indwelling spirits.   The Vais consider themselves surrounded by the spirits of their dead and other spirits which can change themselves into living creatures and other objects, and which actually do evil to the individual and the tribe.   The Vais consider it therefore their first duty to satisfy and protect themselves against these spirits, and in doing so they think they are serving their God.   Their religious life and practice seem to be limited to the native medicine, the various amulets, the fetiches, and the sacrifices that are deemed by them adapted to the discharge of their first duty.   But behind and apart from all amulets, fetiches, and sacrifices, the Vais recognize a higher Power, and they call It Karmba, — God.

So far as I have been able to observe the pagan Vais have not as yet risen to the conception of worshiping Karmba apart from any natural object or phenomena.[2] They have always impressed me as being absorbed in protecting themselves in this life against invisible beings and spirits with which their fancy and imagination have peopled the earth.

[2] They call upon Karmba, however, in moments of great distress and pain.

VAI CLOTH, SHOES, IVORY MORTAR, PALM STRAINER, ETC.

Facing Page 86

RELIGIOUS CEREMONIES AND SACRIFICES

We have seen how the Vais honor their dead in a social function.³ We now come to the consideration of the custom of the Vais of associating their dead with religious ceremonies and sacrifices. On account of the belief in spirits and their association with living creatures, material objects, and natural phenomena, sacrifices are made to different things in different sections of the Vai country, for sacrifices to the dead are not local but general. In all the Vai towns once or twice every year after the dead have been buried the remaining relatives visit the grave and carry with them rice, rum, palm butter, and so forth, which are placed near the grave. Then they go through a kind of ceremony in which they chant Vai songs in honor of the dead. They believe that where the dead are it is necessary for them to have food to eat. They think that the dead also need clothes or something to wear, and so they carry to the graves white cloth. All these articles are left at the grave, and it is thought that the spirit of the deceased will come for them. In thus providing for the dead they have the idea that if they do not so provide the spirits will be displeased and punish them for neglect.

The object, therefore, of making sacrifices to the dead is to keep in the favor of the imaginary spirits thereof and thus prosper in life. Special ceremonies and sacrifices are held for the very important men and women of high and ruling families. In these cases as in the others native food and cloth are sacrificed at the grave of the departed, but the ceremonies are much longer and far more impressive because they are participated in by the

³ " Social Functions, Deaths, and Dances," Chapter IV, 6.

people generally, and sometimes extend beyond the limits of towns and provinces.

We are thus brought to the consideration of another class of religious sacrifices,— a class which may be called local, because they grow out of the environment of a particular locality. For example, in localities where the palm-tree flourishes sacrifices of a religious nature are made to palm-trees. When there is a scarcity of palm nuts, before the next palm nut season the chief of the locality where the scarcity exists selects a certain palm-tree, and on an appointed day the people are called to the palm grove and sacrifices are made to the tree selected. The sacrifices are accompanied by a ceremony, with singing and drum beating. Certain medicine is placed on this tree and no one may gather palm nuts from it without suffering severe penalties. This tree is regarded with the greatest esteem. The reason for this sacrifice to this palm-tree is that the Vais believe that some one of the palm-trees, through its indwelling spirit, controls the rest. They think the spirit of the tree, being displeased, prevented the other palm-trees from bearing palm nuts, so they endeavor to secure its good-will by sacrifices. The palm-tree selected [4] is the one which gives the impression that it contains the dominant spirit.

Along the rivers where alligators are plentiful and do violence to the people sacrifices of chickens, rum, rice, and so on are made to them. All along the shores of Lake Peso the alligators at one time were very destructive to human life, and the town of Sugary is now noted for having alligators that are kept as pets and witches and that are believed to be the possessors of evil spirits. We

[4] Palm-tree the most important tree to native life, see Chapter III, "Economic Life of the Vais," 2, "Natural Products," etc.

have mentioned the alligator in its connection with witch-craft.[5] In certain localities, on account of its great menace to and destruction of native life, the Vais have connected it with the evil spirit, and they believe that it must have sacrifices made to it in order to appease its anger and to keep it in a friendly mood.

In this connection I am reminded of a Vai legend involving the principle of sacrifice. During the early settlement of Manna Salijah, a section of the Manna country, King Salee ruled. To-day the country bears the name of this king Salijah. It is said that the alligators were very troublesome there. The natives were afraid to fish, and two or three persons were destroyed a day. Numbers of persons were missing every week. The annoyance and dread became very great. Finally one of the old men had a dream.

The old man said he dreamed that the alligators were very angry and wanted the favorite of the king, the son he loved best; nothing less would appease their anger; that this sacrifice would be followed by general prosperity; that regularly the steamers would call at Manna, trade would revive, and the people become rich. This dream was made known to the king and all his subjects. King Salee was sad but willing to make any sacrifice to save and enrich his people. He sought his favorite son, Vahnee Bamblu, told him the dream, and asked if he would willingly sacrifice his life to the alligators. The son consented, and was promised anything he desired for three weeks. The king called together all his subjects to a big feast, and until the day for the sacrifice the revelry of eating, drinking, and dancing continued, with the music of horns, sasas, and the beating of drums.

[5] See 5. "Scope and Influence of Witchcraft," Chapter IV.

In the meantime a beautiful maiden was taken from the "Greegree Bush" and given to Vahnee Bamblu. Every wish of his was gratified. His head, neck, and limbs were decorated with jewelry of silver and gold; his fingers were adorned with rings; shoes were placed upon his feet; he was donned in the most beautiful clothes, and was carried about in a hammock. He was attended by numerous servants who honored him and were ready to satisfy his every wish. The day for the sacrifice arrived. Vahnee Bamblu was bathed, clad in the finest clothes, dressed with the rarest jewels, and after midday was placed in a canoe, carried to the center of the river, and with heavy weights sunk to the bottom thereof.

At that moment a loud report resembling the roar of a cannon was heard sounding from below. It was so terrific that many persons on shore were frightened. The sound was interpreted to mean that the anger of the alligators was appeased and they were to enjoy general prosperity. The people had great rejoicing. From that day the people of Salee were no more troubled nor destroyed by the alligators. Frequently steamers called and Manna became a large commercial port. The belief is common that if any of the descendants of King Salee or any residents of Manna Salijah are capsized and are attacked by an alligator, they have only to mention the name of Vahnee Bamblu, and the alligator will do them no harm.

Very recently another old man had a dream. To him Vahnee Bamblu appeared, saying that he, Vahnee Bamblu, had become too old and that they must send some one else in his place, if they would enjoy better prosperity and become very rich. This dream is being widely circulated in the Vai country, but no active step is known to have been taken to make another sacrifice to relieve Vahnee Bamblu.

To all the descendants of King Salee and his country this legend is told, and it is believed by them to be a fact.

Now we are to glance at a class of religious sacrifices that are both general and local; general in the sense that no locality is exempt from the operation of the clauses which give rise to the sacrifices, and local in that they are usually limited to a definite area at one time. I refer to the sacrifices to the spirits which control natural phenomena, such as lightning, droughts, thunder, and so on. When a drought destroys the crops the Vais conclude that some spirit is displeased. The most mysterious place near the fields is thought to be the habitat of this angered spirit. The people are called together to go to this place and there make the usual native sacrifice in the customary manner.

When lightning strikes a house or tree near a town the object struck is thought to contain the displeased spirit, and a sacrifice is offered to it. I recall an illustration of this belief in the Vai town of Manjama. I arrived at this town on the afternoon of May 1, 1904. About 4 P. M. I told the carriers to get some wood to make a fire with which to cook dinner. They got the wood, but the chief of the town took the wood from them and had it carried outside the town. He declared that the wood could not be burned in his town. Upon inquiry I found a door frame had been made of it for a house and that the lightning had struck it. The chief showed me the house with its shattered door frame. He told of the sacrifice to the spirit dwelling in the wood and pointed out his medicine fastened thereon, which he had placed there to cause God to keep the lightning out of his town.

When I was about to take a canoe at Cape Mount to go to the extreme end of the lake known as Peso Lake, I had places pointed out to me where many persons had lost their lives when the lake was rough. Nearly all the rivers have places where persons are often capsized and drowned. The Vais believe that there are certain water spirits which live in the water and when displeased drown persons traversing the river or lake. At these particular places sacrifices are offered to keep these spirits in a friendly mood so that they will trouble no one. The natives make a sacrifice of a white plate, a white chicken, and a white piece of cloth. Should the canoe be about to capsize they believe that to drop the foregoing articles into the water will be sufficient to save them from harm and death.

THE RELIGIOUS FUNCTION OF THE MEDICINE-MAN

The medicine-man is a very important man. There are several classes of them. The importance of each medicine-man usually depends upon the class to which he belongs. In some way he is connected with almost everything, and in matters of religion he seems an indispensable factor. The mention of two classes will be sufficient for the present purpose. The head of the beri, called a beri-mo, belongs to the highest class of medicine-men. He has great political power, and is held in so great esteem that very few may see him. During the time that the youths are in the beri they are not only taught regarding the laws and matters of the Government but they are given instruction in religious duties, ceremonies, and sacrifices to the various spirits thought to bring good or ill fortune upon the Vai people. When, according to the instructions of the beri-mo, certain medicine is placed on a palm-tree, no one is supposed to gather palm nuts from or otherwise to interfere with this tree except under the pains and penalties of death.

The violation of the religious laws is a very serious matter, and the beri-mo visits upon the violator certain death. These medicine-men meet in their council and decide the punishment and the manner of its infliction. They are never known by the people. Generally some one in the family is instructed to execute the judgment. I am reliably informed by high Vai authority that death is generally inflicted by poisoning. It is said that a member of the family is commissioned to execute the sentences of the beri-mo-men in order to keep the tribe together and prevent dissensions. Husbands kill their wives, sisters their brothers, and wives their husbands. Any person, a near relative, is liable to be selected for this work. No one can refuse; to refuse is death. And thus the sight of the medicine of the beri-mo is quite sufficient to secure the religious respect for which it is intended.

In contrast to this beri-mo, who is intensely serious, is the common medicine-man. His religious services may be obtained for his fee. If one is sick, for his fee he will, through his medicine, invoke the good offices of the invisible spirits. The belief is common that he can cure sickness in this way. I have heard of mány instances where sick persons were told by this medicine-man to sacrifice a white chicken, to give away a white piece of cloth, and so on, and the patients did it and were restored to health immediately. The farmer who plants his farm, — which is open and exposed to any thief who may desire to steal from it,— consults the medicine-man, pays his fee, and gets medicine which, when placed upon a tree or bush near-by and seen by the thief, will cause him to drop the objects of his theft. The mourners visiting the graves of their loved ones with tokens of affection and religious sacrifice may leave with these objects a bit of medicine from the medicine-man, wrapt apparently in a common rag, that will protect them all from the hand extended to defile the grave.

This medicine-man represents himself as being in communion with and controlling the ruling spirits. His medicine is good for all the ills common to the native life. Among the other tribes,— like the Gora, Basá, and p esi, unless they are trained under the Mandingoes or Vais,— the medicine-man is little more than a herb doctor. The industrious Mandingoes have sent their teachers among all the tribes between them and the coast. In no particular is their influence more visible than in the added functions of the medicine-man. It is now common to see the medicine-men traveling in Liberia, for they can secure practice and succeed when most other men would fail.[6] Often with the practice of medicine is combined the function of the priest, and in all their religious work among the people the great and all-important doctrine is sacrifice, and this is the key to the pagan religious life of the Vais.

ISLAMIC FAITH AMONG THE VAIS

The history of Islam in West Africa is very interest-

[6] " These Mori men certainly make more money than anyone else in the country, as they do nothing without being handsomely paid for it. They are the sole purveyors of the written fetiches. Everybody wears some sort of fetich or greegree, and of course everybody has to pay for it." " The Sherbro and Its Hinterland," by T. J. Alldridge, F.R.G.S., p. 105.

VAI ISLAMIC MOSQUE

ing. The weight of authority is to the effect that it probably crossed the Sahara about the eleventh century, A. D., although the Tarik, a history of the Western Sudan written in the 17th century by Amir Es Sardi, contains a reference to a prince of the Songhai Kingdom, who about 1000 A. D., became a follower of Muhammud. Upon the authority of Leo Africanus we believe that many Negroes accepted the tenets of Muhammud during the reign of Yusif Iben Tashfin, the founder of Morocco, as early at 1062 A. D. [7]   Dr. Barth, a German traveler, ascribes the introduction of Islam into Bornu to the year 1086, during the reign of Hume, who perhaps died on his way to or from the city of Mecca. Mr. Morel, an authority on West African Affairs, is of the opinion that Islam was in the region of the Senegal about the 9th century A. D.,[8] and pressed eastward, reaching Gao on the Niger near the opening of the 11th century, and continued in a triumphal march to the great Negro kingdom of Kanem. Others contend that Islam came to the Sudan from the eastward. But whichever way it came, it came and from without, and was felt among the Negroes of the Niger Bend in the 11th century; and,— upon such eminent authorities as Morel, Dubois, Blyden, and others,— Islam became an important factor in the religious faith and practice of the finer Negroes of the continent. It is said that throughout the northern portions of Africa the Koran, its sacred book, is read from the "Atlantic to the Red Sea, and from the Mediterranean to the Congo." Dr. Blyden, in the following words, well likened its phases to the English drum-beat described so poetically by Daniel Webster:

[7] "Christianity, Islam, and the Negro Race," by Dr. Blyden, p. 6.
[8] "Affairs of West Africa," by E. D. Morel, p. 210.

" They keep company with the hours, and from lofty minarets encircle the globe with one unbroken strain of the mellifluous sounds of Arabia,— Allahu Akbar, Allahu Akbar." [9]

Islam is a potent force in the religious life of the Vais. Whether the Vais accepted this faith before or since they came to the coast it is impossible to say. The Rev. S. W. Koelle said fifty years ago that not more than one-fourth of them were Muhammudans. The number is much larger now.· A Christian missionary at Cape Mount estimates that 95 per cent. of the Vais are Muslims.[10]   In most of the towns and some of the half-towns the Muhammudans have schools and mosques, and they are generally regarded as being somewhat superior to their pagan brothers.   In the schools the boys are taught Arabic, and some of them become quite proficient in it. Instruction is given in this language in order that the Koran and other works in Arabic may be read.   In the mosques the adherents of Islam may be seen praying five times a day, but wherever they are they pray before sunrise, at noon, in the afternoon, in the evening, and just at night.   It is said that when praying Muhammud turned his face to the West,—

" Because," as he said, " from that quarter crowds will enter the religion of Islam and be among the most faithful of its adherents." [11]

[9] " The Koran in Africa," by Dr. E. W. Blyden, in the *Journal of the African Society*, January, 1905.
[10] Miss Agnes P. Mahoney in a conversation and in a letter gave me this estimate in April, 1905, and later.
[11] " The Koran in Africa," by Dr. Blyden, in *Journal of the African Society*, p. 158.

Admirably the prophecy has been fulfilled. But the Vais in praying turn their faces to the East toward Kaaba, a sacred shrine in Mecca, believed to be a special gift of God and the favorite praying-place of Ishmael and Abraham. Some of the Vai Mussulmen are very devoted to their faith, which seems to possess their whole hearts. For thirty days they hold the annual fast of Ramadhan, at the close of which they celebrate the festival of Bairam. For hours I have listened to them gathered in a group, and with one person as a leader, chanting from memory the sacred lines of the Koran.

There has been a great deal of discussion as to the character and effect of Islamism. One writer describes it in these words:

" Islamism is in itself stationary, and was framed thus to remain; sterile like its God, lifeless like its first principle in all that constitutes life,— for life is love, participation, and progress, and of these the Koranic deity has none. It justly repudiates all change, all development; to borrow the forcible words of Lord Houghton, the written book is there the dead man's hand, stiff and motionless; whatever savours of vitality is by that alone convicted of heresy and defection." [12]

Doubtless the writer of this passage had in mind the effect of Islamism in Arabia, and it will hardly be disputed that there is some truth in what he says so far as the effect of Muhammudanism upon mankind in general is concerned. But when we come to the Negro in Africa the description is in violent contradiction to the fact. That Islamism is an important factor in improving the

[12] Palgrave's "Arabia," Vol. I, p. 372.

morals of the Negro and in civilizing him has been most
ably proved by such forceful writers as Thompson and
Taylor, Reclus and Morel, Bosworth Smith, and Dr.
Blyden. Speaking of the influence of the Arabian faith
upon its entrance into the Sudan, Mr. Morel gives this
important testimony of Joseph Thompson:

" Under the fostering impulse and care of the new
religion these backward regions commenced an upward
progress." [13]

Mr. Thompson's testimony cannot be brushed aside without reason, for about 1884 he visited that portion of Negroland now known as Northern Nigeria, and he has been
described by so voluminous a writer as Noble as

" a scientific observer and the humanest, the noblest of
African explorers since Livingstone." [14]

Mr. Bosworth Smith is a remarkable Englishman in
that he pored over the pages of the Koran and over the
works of African travelers and savants until he was not
only able to appreciate the spirit of Islam but to enter
into it

" in a manner which," as Dr. Blyden says, " but
for the antecedent labors of Lane, Sprenger, Deutsch,
and Weil, would be astounding in a Western scholar and
Englishman." [15]

[13] "Affairs of West Africa," by E. D. Morel, p. 211. "Mungo
Park," by Joseph Thompson in the "World's Greatest Explorers"
series. Mr. Morel's book contains two of the strongest chapters
ever written in favor of the influence of Islam on the Negro.
[14] "Redemption of Africa," by Noble, Vol. I, p. 68.
[15] "Christianity, Islam, and the Negro Race," by Dr. Blyden, p. 3.

Mr. Smith, while lecturing in 1874 at the Royal Institution of Great Britain weighed and described the effect of the Muslim faith on the Negro with much of the accuracy of one who had spent some time in observation and study on the ground. He says:

" Christian travelers, with every wish to think otherwise, have remarked that the negro who accepts Muhammudanism acquires at once a sense of the dignity of human nature not commonly found even among those who have been brought to accept Christianity." [16]

Yet, as just as Mr. Smith tried to be and was in discussing the Negro, the above passage shows that in some respects he still had the prejudice against which he so gallantly fought. He began the name of the black race with a small " n."   And like so many of the present-day writers he was unable to see, as Dr. Blyden pointed out long ago, that the word Negro is entitled to the same distinction as Hindoo, Indian, and other race names, and that it is the height of inconsistency to write Congo, Vai, Basa, Mandingo, and Ashantee with capitals and " negro " with a small letter.[17]   For when did the parts become greater than the whole?

The Géographie Universelle of M. Elisée Reclus is a classic in African literature. By it he " made the scientific world debtor for a vast treasure-house of natural science in its African aspects and relations." [18] The author of this very valuable and important work speaks of the influence of Islam on the Negro in these words:

[16] " Muhammud and Muhammudanism," by R. B. Smith, Lecture I, p. 32.
[17] " Christianity, Islam, and the Negro Race," by Dr. Blyden, p. 11, in a note.
[18] " Redemption of Africa," by Noble, author's note, Vol. I, p. 11.

"In Nigretia the propagation of Islam coincides with important political and social changes. Large states were founded in regions hitherto a prey to a hundred hostile savage tribes. Manners softened. Solidarity sprang up between communities formerly engaged in ceaseless war. Muhammudanism enjoys more material cohesion than in Asia. . . . Their common belief tends everywhere to diffuse the social ideas, habits, usages and speech of the Arab. . . . At Mecca the most zealous pilgrims, those subject to most frequent fits of religious frenzy, are the Negroes of Wadai and Bornu and the inhabitants of northwest Abyssinia. Notwithstanding the difficulties of the journey, thousands of Tekrurs undertake the pilgrimage every year. In West Africa the propagators of Islam are Negroes." [19]

There is no question but what M. Reclus is an able scholar. He was twenty years preparing what is now regarded as the most complete geography of the world. And it is extremely unlikely that a man, after the most extensive traveling, one endowed with the qualifications to render such eminent services to the world of science, would attribute to Islam a false effect on the Negro, contrary to conventional opinion, and describe it with such force and minuteness, unless his opinion had been determined by the most convincing facts. The rejection of his statement requires either the disclosure of his ignorance or the impeachment of his character. As yet neither has been done.

Dr. Blyden, the eminent Negro scholar, wrote in *Frazer's Magazine* in 1875:

"Muhammudanism in Africa counts in its ranks the

[19] "Redemption of Africa," by Noble, Vol. I, p. 68.

most energetic and enterprising tribes. It claims as adherents the only people who have any form of social polity or bond of social organization. It has built and occupies the largest cities in the heart of the continent. Its laws regulate the most powerful kingdoms,— Futah, Masina, Hausa, Bornu, Wadai, Dafur, Kordofan, Senaar, etc." [20]

Thirty years afterwards, describing the sway of the Koran in Africa, this distinguished writer said:

" If there were a railway from West Africa to the Red Sea, and you wished to avail yourself of it to journey to Egypt during the fast (you might accomplish the journey perhaps in seven days), you would during those seven days pass through a region where you would find every man, woman, and child in good health observing the fast. On the entire route,— 4000 miles,— you would notice that the fires were out in the daytime. Sixty millions of people fasting at the same time! I believe that more than one-half of these are Negroes." [21]

More than thirty years ago Dr. Blyden was not only a scholar but had

" enjoyed exceptional advantages for observation and comparison in the United States, the West Indies, South America, Egypt, Syria, West and Central Africa."

As Director of the Department of Muhammudan Education at Sierra Leone he has had the most favorable

[20] " Christianity, Islam, and the Negro Race," by Dr. Blyden, p. 6.
[21] " The Koran in Africa," by Dr. Blyden in *Journal of the African Society,* January, 1905.

opportunities for ascertaining the influence of Islam on the Negro Muslims. And with a scholarship further broadened and enriched with thirty years of study and observation of life and letters in Africa and the world, Dr. Blyden speaks on this question with an authority which must command respect if it does not force convietion.

M. Dubois, the author of " Timbuctu the Mysterious," who while traveling in the Sudan secured some very valuable manuscripts,[22] used these words respecting the Negroes of this portion of Africa:

" We possess the biographies of several hundred of these learned men, and all are related to one another in a more or less direct line. A cerebral refinement was thus produced among a certain proportion of the Negraic population which has had surprising results, as we shall see later, and which gives the categorical lie to the theorists who insist upon the inferiority of the black races." [23]

Against the facts presented by such distinguished writers we have the views of just as splendid a line of able men,— like Blerzey, Church, Noble, Renan, and Freeman,— men who have formed their conclusions mainly from the observations of others, and who have not traveled and therefore have not studied the African and his institutions in Africa as much and as long as have Thompson, Dubois, and Blyden. But their conclusions in many respects are sound, and their distance has enabled them to bring to their works a charm which perhaps a closer view would obscure. Mr. Noble tries to

[22] First complete copy of the Tarik, a history of Sudan.
[23] " Timbuctu the Mysterious," by Dubois, p. 278.

take a very liberal interpretation of the Negro, and M. Renan is renowned for his trenchant criticisms. A citation from each of them will be sufficient to indicate the general opinion of all these men. The influence of Islam is summed up by Renan as follows:

" On ground none of the best Islam has done as much harm as good. It has stifled everything by its arid and desolating simplicity. . . . The essential condition of a diffused civilization is the destruction of Islam. The product of an inferior and meager combination of human elements, its conquests have all been on the average plane. Savage races have been incapable of rising to it. It has not satisfied the people who carried in themselves the seeds of a stronger civilization." [24]

As applied to man generally this seems to express the trend and the weight of opinion among those competent to judge. In this opinion Mr. Noble agrees, and after, as he says, turning " from the polemics of partisans such as missionaries, theologians, and travelers," and in the light of history examining the works of such students and scholars as August Mueller, Theodor Noeldeke, Wilhelm Spitta, Dean Stanley, and Wellhausen, he proceeds to judge the worth and the work of Islam in Africa. And after portraying the merits and defects of Islam as an African Missionary, he states among his conclusions the following opinions:

" Islam has been slow in operation, superficial and unsatisfying in actual achievements. Its African conquests, though larger in area than Europe, cost nearly thirteen

[24] " Redemption of Africa," quoted by F. P. Noble, Vol. I, p. 66.

hundred years of effort, are more nominal than real, and relatively number but few adherents. As an ethical, spiritual, and state-building force it has proved a failure. In Egypt, North Africa, and Northern Sahara it supplanted a superior civilization; in Sudan the Muslim brought a culture little if any superior to that of the Negro. In the lands of the Negro the Muslim success consists of Arab immigration; the conversion of five or six influential tribes; and their conquests of others."

It is said that Islam requires no change of heart or life, that its acceptance is made easy by the simplicity and poverty of its creed, and that its social force is greater than its spiritual potency. They say that when charged with political authority the spirit of Islam is military, and the missionary spirit was just born in the 19th century;[25] that the Koran teems with commands to fight, that the distinctive feature of Islam is the Holy War, and that this faith regards the sword as the best missionary. With the force of truth it is observed that Islam makes concessions to Negro beliefs, substitutes the Muslim minister for the pagan medicine-man, and replaces the native fetiches with Koranic verses as amulets. Yet, after all, Mr. Morel, who as editor of the *West African Mail* must keep in touch with conditions and life in West Africa, makes the following significant statement:

"Individually and collectively the Negro has progressed since Islam crossed the desert, and just as to the

[25] Page 219, "Affairs of West Africa." This is contradicted by Mr. Morel, who is one of the ablest living authorities on West Africa. His chapters on "Islam in West Africa" are exceedingly strong and interesting.

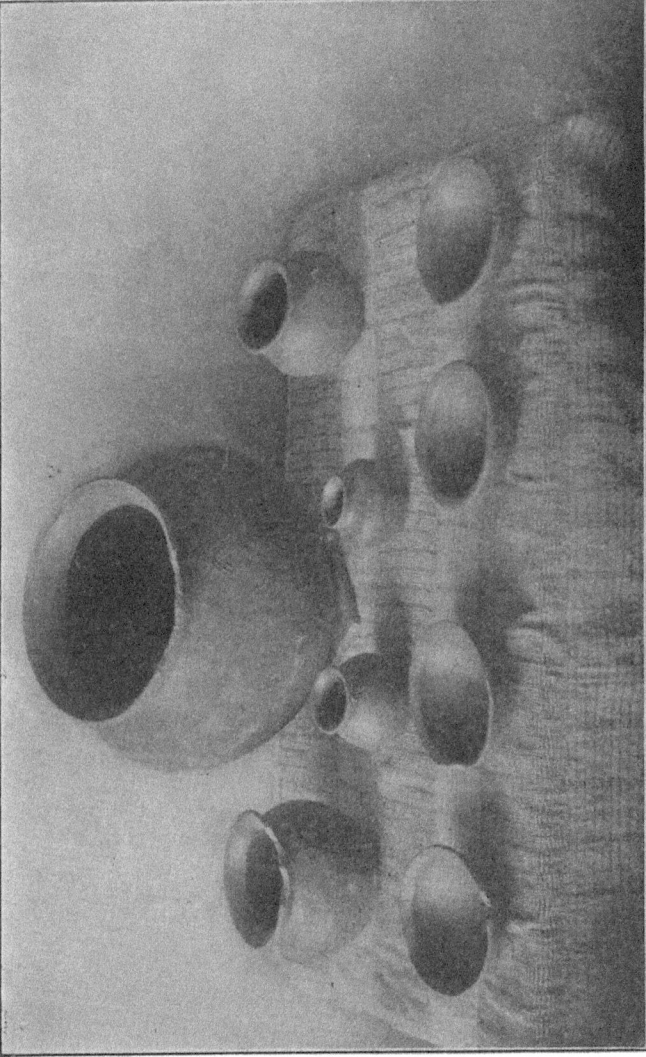

NATIVE VAI CROCKERY

Facing Page 104

Negro fetich of the forest and the swamp religious conceptions permeate every act, preside over every undertaking, and insinuate themselves into every incident of his daily existence, so Islam, while it has laid permanent hold upon the Negro, claims from him an allegiance entire and complete." [26]

He cites the authority of a clergyman of the Church Missionary Society who describes

" a ceaseless stream of Hausa pilgrims continually passing through Tripoli on the way to Mecca after a wearisome tramp across the desert,"

and reminds us of that larger but still " ceaseless stream " of Negroes from all parts of Western Africa which pours across the drifting and scorching sands of the Sahara for the precious sight of Mecca. It matters but little if the Fulah, Mandingo, Yolof, Egypto-Sudanese followers, and Zanzibari Muhammudans have records as warriors; or that Islam is discredited from Kartum to Wadelai by Felkin and Wilson, with the Hausas by Barth, the Futa highlander and Mandinges by Lenz, and the Bambara and Yolof by Brun-Renand; the evidences and authorities are increasing that among the Negroes of Western Africa Islam, with all its faults, and it has many, is an important factor where it has taken root. It does not do what Christianity would do if it were embraced and established to the same extent, but the Muhammudan Negro is a great improvement on the pure pagan. I have been able to observe the Basás, Goras, p esi, and other pagan tribes in Liberia, and in industrial skill, self-respect, energy, and intellectual attain-

[26] "Affairs of West Africa," by E. D. Morel, p. 212.

ments they are inferior to the Vais and Mandingo Muslims.

I may be unduly influenced by the fact that I found a Negro Mussulman within easy reach of Monrovia with nearly 150 volumes in Arabic, covering a wide range of subjects.[27] Fifty of these volumes were by Negro authors, who wrote concerning law, theology, music, science, grammar, rhetoric, and medicine. I venture to give the list as I obtained it.

I. SCIENCE

Ah da ma boo noo oo roo soo oo le, Treatise on Animal Life.

2. GRAMMAR

Gya roo ma and Ma e da ne you.

3. RHETORIC

Ba na too soo an doo,[28] Na fe an too too labe,[29] Ah la sa me sa me, La ta ah le ka na na, Alema ka ma too,[30] by Aboale Kassime or Booade-En-Gade.

4. MEDICINE

Sa noo soo ahle ma roo fe,[31] Tale ya koo,[32] Sa ma wate,[33] and Ba too ta ne.[34]

[27] Momoru Duclay, the Negro Muslim of Brahma.
[28] Named after wife who had run away.
[29] To help school boy.
[30] Rough rice; one must go to school before he can know it, so rice must be beaten before eaten.
[31] Well-known day.
[32] Path for Medicine.
[33] The Top of all Medicine Books, or the best.
[34] Shelter for God-man.

5. LAW

Lame yata ahle moo ta ra ne mena, School Song Book;
Ah fa ge ah leme se koo, School Law; La an le moo ah
le moo ta an le moo, School Law; La ke la le you, Ba
ha ge, Koo roo te be you and Noo boola soo.

6. MUSIC

Wa te le yate, Boo noo boo oo la de, Ah boo se le,
Gi noo al le anbe de na, Gya ge na an ba, Ba da ma se,
Na soo ka de, Sa ra too laha be, Ba ah boo la, Ya la
besa, Da le ya, Sake fa alle ho dah,[35] by Qua ge ba fama,
Boo le da ta ke me so, by Mu ham mu di Mal i kaise you,
Boo le ba ha mo gya oo, same author.

7. THEOLOGY

La se le tan,[36] Too lane gu loo la ma,[37] Na se ha too,[38]
Wa ka la se you, Se too wa se too na,[39] Ha se boo ah le
ha sa na te, Na se ha too ah le fa ta ha,[40] Fa ma an na,
Ma ah koo too moo ahn,[41] Ya moo an ta wa ha de,[42] Soo
ke la, Koo boo ra, Ya ra ro dene,[43] Soo la me, Sa ya
la ta ah le gya kene, Ja wa ha la,[44] and Ya koo loo sa
ekoo na.

[35] Divided into ten parts.
[36] Means difficult to learn; compared to bullock with short neck, difficult to catch.
[37] Means that the book will make glad those who read it.
[38] Sixty-six parts.
[39] Young Boy Glad.
[40] Twenty parts.
[41] Means all theology included in this book.
[42] Means the book is the best on theology.
[43] The diamond of all theological works, that is the best.
[44] The sayings of the minister of the Gospel.

It is very improbable that Negroes would master Arabic,[45] a foreign language, with such proficiency as to enable them to write books in this alien tongue,— and books on such varied subjects,— without being themselves impressed not only by the language but by the literature thereof. Glance over this list of books and it will disclose just what would naturally be of interest to the Negroes to whom Arabian culture had been brought through the missionary and military efforts of Islam. There are seven books on law, five on science and medicine, seven on grammar and rhetoric, fourteen on music, and seventeen on theology. The Negro is well known to be highly musical, and his authorship in this line, as far as this Muslim library discloses it, shows that he made this Arabian language pay tribute to his nature and respond to his pleasure. But great as seems to be the tendency of the Negro to write about music,— a subject that is naturally interesting to him,— he appears to be even more given to writing about theology. The Koran inspired the learning of Arabic and the questions considered therein would of course for some time attract a great number of the proselyted people.

Mr. Draper, speaking of Europe's obligation to the Muhammudans,[46] says:

" I have to deplore the systematic manner in which the literature of Europe has contrived to put out of sight our scientific obligations to the Muhammudans." And he adds, " Surely they cannot be much longer hidden."

[45] Please note that the foregoing African names in Arabic are written for the first time by the writer, and not having seen them written before he cannot vouch for the correctness of the spelling.

[46] "Intellectual Development of Europe," by J. W. Draper, Vol. I, p. 42.

As true as this assertion is in regard to the Muslim, literature has treated the Negro even worse. Both Europe and America have concealed to a great extent the Negro's part in the civilizations of Africa and the world. But " surely they cannot be much longer hidden." And, in spite of certain literary critics, we must conclude that Islam exercises a powerful grip on the Negro mind. Originally the propagators of the Meccan faith were Berber and Arabic Mussulmen. And although now the same faith is chiefly spread by Negroes in West Africa, I have seen among the Vais Arabic Muslims with their Negro wives.

The Vais entertain the deepest veneration for the Koran. Those who profess the faith of the Meccan prophet evince a superiority over their pagan tribesmen and possess a zeal, dignity, and devotion which at least are impressive. The Vai Negro's attachment to the Islamic faith is not without cause, for they are taught that the Negro has an honorable part in the military history and noted achievements of the religion. By the best informed Muhammudans the Africans are made to feel a pride in the fact that their race is recognized in the Koran, which contains a chapter inscribed to a Negro,[47] and that Muhammud was in part descended from an African and had a Negro as a confidant in Arabia. It is pointed out that Negroes figured prominently in the progress of Islam, and on one occasion slew a rival of Muhammud. It is said that the prophet greatly admired a Negro poet of anti-Islamic times, and regretted that he had never seen him.

The Vai Negroes thus feel a close relationship to the

[47] Logman, Chapter 31, Koran, Steingrass's translation of "The Assemblies of Harire," Vol. II, p. 245, by Dr. E. W. Blyden.

Koranic faith. As we have seen they name their children after Muhammud and the prophets as if they were their kinsmen. They delight to think of and commune with the great masters of their faith as equals. Their boys may be seen writing in the sand these names and the words of the Koran. With all the pride of distinguished ancestors, with the names and memory of great Negroes, renowned in the military history and progress of Islam, and with all the inspiration which a knowledge of the Koran and its language gives, their scholars and priests go forth daily to teach and to widen the influence of Islam among their pagan fellows, without money and without price. The followers and adherents of Muhammud can easily be distinguished from the pagan Vais. Among this people the Arabian faith is a vital, living, active force. It stirs the spiritual nature of the Vai-speaking Negro to its very depths.[48]

CHRISTIANITY AMONG THE VAIS

The seeds of Christianity are being sown among the Vais. The indications are that they are taking root. For perhaps more than two centuries the Vais have been in communication with European traders, and now and then they came in contact with Christian influence.[49]

[48] " Careful scientific study has enforced on me, as it has on other students, the recognition that the African mind naturally approaches all things from a spiritual point of view. Low down in culture or high up, his mind works along the line that things happen because of the action of spirit upon spirit; it is an effort for him to think in terms of matter." From " West African Studies," by M. H. Kingsley, p. 386.

[49] " West Africa has been in contact with Christianity for three hundred years, and not one single tribe, as a tribe, has yet become Christian." Dr. E. W. Blyden, in " Christianity, Islam, and the Negro Race," p. 25.

Before the present century the Christian influences must have been very slight. The large Peso Lake at Cape Mount, penetrating far into the interior, gave that place an advantage over many others as a point from which to engage in the traffic of human beings. An important slave-trading center was established there, and for some time the slave-trade flourished with all its horrors. Near the interior limits of this lake I saw at Dátia pieces of guns and the remnants of old cannon, which it was said were furnished the Vais by the Spanish to aid the former in securing captives from the neighboring tribes. But after the death of the slave-trade and the birth of the Liberian colony the Vais began to recognize the importance of peace, and to value the friendship of their neighbors. More and more they began to turn to the arts of legitimate industry. The effect of the destruction of the trade in slaves was to force the Vais to seek the extension of their commercial relations with their former foes.

So that about 1860 the Rev. Daniel Ware, an Americo-Liberian, felt safe in settling at Cape Mount, and took into his family some Vai boys and girls. To them he gave instruction in written and spoken English. But unfortunately for the children the Reverend Ware was not long at Cape Mount before he was called to a charge on the St. Paul River near the capital of Liberia. In 1877, under Bishop C. C. Penick, the first organized effort was made to Christianize the Vais, and the St. John Mission was established at Cape Mount by the authority and under the supervision of the Protestant Episcopal Church in the United States. Momolu Masaquoi,[50] a Vai prince formerly at Ghendima, Gallinas, and now at

[50] See 1, " Nature and Form of Government," Chapter V.

Monravia, Liberia, speaking of the condition of the Vais at the founding of the St. John Mission, said:

" In 1877 there were not five men in the Vai territory who spoke decent English: to-day hundreds of young men and women express themselves well in that language. In that year there was not a single man who could read the Roman characters: to-day nearly all business letters, petitions, and other diplomatic documents from Vai kings and merchants are written by Vai boys and girls in civilized language. In 1877 there was not a single Christian among us: to-day we have hundreds in the fold of Christ." [51]

Besides, the St. John Mission has sent out many Vai boys and girls who are now in the civilized settlements of Liberia. I saw a goodly number in various towns in the Vai country. Many Vai boys from this Mission are now filling clerkships and other positions along the West Coast. And others yet have made and are now making splendid records in the institutions for higher learning in the United States and Europe. I have had the pleasure of visiting this Mission under the supervision of the Right Reverend Bishop S. D. Ferguson, and I know that it has rendered efficient and valuable services to the Vai people and the Republic of Liberia. These services have been so marked and so valuable that they elicited words of commendation from President Arthur Barclay in his first inaugural address.[52]

The enrolment of the St. John Mission for 1904, as reported by the Right Reverend Bishop, was ninety native

[51] The April *Century Magazine*, 1905.
[52] Inaugural Address of President Barclay, January, 1904.

Vai children and ten Liberians. Therefore the chief work of the school is among the natives where it is most needed. The continued progress of this Mission and the establishment of Christian schools in the heart and interior of the Vai country will be interesting to persons who feel a lively concern in the question raised by those who have so powerfully pleaded the cause of Islam for the Negro.

It is deeply regretted that the present consideration of this very interesting question would carry us outside the scope of our thesis. Nevertheless, we cannot resist the temptation to say that for centuries the Vais have been sitting at the feet of Mandingan and Arabic scholars who are laden with Koranic wisdom and who possess some of the principles and classic lore of Oriental civilization. The language of the Koran has opened to the Vais another world of life and letters superior to their own. In many towns for generations Vai scholars have drilled into Vai children the knowledge and culture of the Koran. Social sympathy, personal and racial pride, have all been invoked to attach the Vais to the prophet of Mecca. Throughout the tribe the standard of Islam has been unfurled. While the sway of the Koran has done something for the Vais, still they are a prey to the evils of the polygamic marriage and the African labor system. Among them, except where modified by Liberian influence, the baneful institution of domestic slavery still stalks unchallenged, with all its withering and blighting features. And while the fetiches have changed their form, the Vai Muhammudan still wears them and still believes in their protecting grace.

Judging from the results of the St. John Mission at Cape Mount, which has only been operating a little over a quarter of a century, the indications are that the Vais are capable in every way of grasping the principles of Christianity and of absorbing the facts and the culture of Modern Civilization. It seems only a question of time when the Church shall have prepared the Vais with teachers and preachers of their own tribe. The people are eager to learn and to send their children to school. And if ever they are enabled to educate them in their own towns according to modern methods and along modern lines, the high order of Vai capacity ought to achieve for the Vai-speaking peoples a creditable place in Christian Civilization. Any one of the great modern languages will open to this people a wealth of life and learning, the dominant note of which is individual and social development. Science, literature, art, philosophy, and Christianity will do for the Vais what they have done for the nations,— that is, enable them to utilize their natural resources and to actualize their highest social and spiritual destiny. An industrial school was established at Ghendima in 1900. Some of the forces of Civilization have entered the field. The contest is submitted to the future. The great difficulty will be to provide Christianity and Modern Civilization with Vai roots in the Vai country. But once this is done the Crescent must wane before the Cross.

NATIVE DEVIL PARADE

CHAPTER VII

STANDARD OF MORALS AMONG THE VAIS

BEFORE AND AFTER MARRIAGE

IT is a common opinion that among the young of the Africans the standard of morals is very high. This is especially true where the African is under his own institutions and is uninfluenced from without. We can somewhat understand why this is true. According to the institutions of the African, the greatest caution is taken for the protection of the morals of the young, and particularly the morals of the females. The little girls are taken at or about the ages of eight and ten years and placed in the institution of the " Greegree Bush," and there they remain until they are ready to be married.[1]

Among the Vais the institution in which the girls are placed is called sande. No male is permitted to visit or go within the limits of this institution. The common belief is that if any man violates this law he will suffer death. The native men are positively afraid to approach the limits of the " Greegree Bush," or sande. The native man is impressed that he will die, but just how he does not know. Certain medicine is placed up where it can be seen on the path leading to the institution, and

[1] They may be taken out by parents, but afterward the strictest watch is kept over the girls all the time.

when it is seen by a male he will flee from the place as quickly as possible.   He believes that if he does not do so the medicine will " witch " him and bring death upon him.   I am informed that when a male violates this law the beri-mo of the " Devil Bush " simply has the violator poisoned by a member of his family.   Among the natives native authority and institutions must be respected, and the death of some civilized persons is attributed to the violation of native laws and defiance to native institutions or authority, relative to the beri or sande societies.

The Vais being on the coast and coming in contact with foreign influences, those nearest the line have had their morals weakened so that some of the young girls are never placed in the sande.   The ease with which violators can escape when near civilized settlements is another influence which tends to weaken the institutions for the moral protection of the young.   Foreign civilization very often presents its weakest and evil side, and strong temptations and inducements are held out to the Vais for their young maidens, many of whom are very attractive, and it is a matter to be regretted that some of the Vais are unable to resist them.   So that I think it can be said with truth that the regulations for the protection of the morals of the young are not as strong and stringent nor as effective along the coast and near civilized centers as they are farther into the interior where the institutions and the sentiments which support them are unimpaired.

Though the morals of the Vais as a people are weakened so far as the protection of the young maidens is concerned, they are more so regarding their protection after marriage, owing to the nature of native institutions.   It is a customary law among the Vais that if a woman leaves her husband and goes to another man, the husband may recover from the man double the amount paid for the wife and the price of all the articles supplied her since marriage. In the interior, where it is very difficult for a native man always to get the amount paid for a wife, the native provision for the protection of the family seems adequate, but on the coast the man can more easily pay what is required, and the protection of the native family is proportionately reduced. Moreover, the native women in the interior have few wants and are exposed to few temptations. When they come in contact with outside influences,— too often evil,— which excite new and varied wants, they become too frequently the prey of that dissatisfaction which impairs the marriage bond and in many instances leads to gross immorality. These are the influences to which the Vai females near the coast towns are subjected. If they are taken into Liberian families when they are young, they are protected in a way from such influences by a course of training for social duties, which training often serves them in married life. But where they are left in the native towns to come in contact with foreign evil influences, without an opportunity to learn the best of civilized life, the baleful effect is plainly seen in the lowering of the standard of morals.

Just as there is a tendency to lower the morals of the Vai females found in the coast towns, there is also seen the same tendency to lower the morals of the males. A Vai boy in the interior at an early age is placed in the beri; the restraints imposed upon him there are such as will generally restrain him in after years, but as soon as the native families come in contact with the influences from the coast towns, they soon begin to think that it is not necessary to place their boys in the beri. One of the results is that the boy takes on the new vices without the new virtues. The ease with which he can .secure malt liquors tempts him to drink, and he grows to manhood with this blighting habit. Along with drinking grows the equally bad habit of gambling. The native idea of property is communistic. He does not possess the high conception of individual ownership that exists among civilized peoples. In the interior the native is restrained by the medicine-man and his institutions; in the coast towns the only restraint is the possibility of being caught. Seeing so many things that he desires, he is tempted to take something not his own, and thus many add the habit of stealing to their other acquired vices.

On the other hand, many natives are able to increase their earnings, and their increased pecuniary strength often leads some of the men to secure the wives of others. And so the men join the women in loosening the marriage relation and in lowering the standard of morals; and just as the natives are led to take up new vices and new crimes, these additions necessarily increase the frequency and diffusion of some of those they already have. So that drinking, gambling, stealing, lying, and immorality increase among the Vais as they approach the coast. The great majority of the people remain loyal to their institutions, but the removal of native institutions in some cases without adequate substitutes has given rise to the evils to which I have called attention. Similar tendencies are noticed in the coast towns among other tribes along the coast. The question has arisen and is frequently discussed by many persons interested in West African affairs as to whether or not European Civilization is injurious to the African.

Because of the tendencies that I have noted among the Vais, it is contended with great force and rare ability that European Civilization is not good for the African. In support of the contention it is pointed out that Africans who have had contact with Europeans are inferior to those who have not had such contact. The physical and moral superiority of the African in the interior is held up as being in striking contrast to the African of the coast towns, who is not so fine a creature either in strength or in morals. It ought not to be denied that the Africans of the interior are superior to the Africans of the coast in morals; nor should it be denied that this inferiority is directly or indirectly due to European contact. It could hardly be otherwise. In all periods of transition the individual suffers but society gains. To me it seems that the great evil of European contact is not so much in the contact as in the failure of the Europeans to provide institutions as effective in governing the African as are the institutions destroyed by this contact. No race, governed as the African, could adopt European Civilization without a transitional period in which it would practically be without effective government, and during which period that race would suffer. The slowness with which Europeans must influence Africans makes this transitional period long in Africa.[2]

As a whole, European contact is not bad *per se;* and in cases where it is bad, far from being an argument against European Civilization it is simply an argument against methods or individuals. Civilization as we understand it,

[2] And this is not counting for mistakes in policy and bad methods in administration.

and as it is defined by the eminent French historian F. P. G. Guizot, is good for the African if he can only get it.

"Two facts, then," says M. Guizot, in speaking of civilization, " are comprehended in this great fact; it subsists on two conditions: the development of social activity, and that of individual activity; the progress of society and the progress of humanity." [3]

History affords no illustration where such a civilization injured any people. If it injures the African he will be the first. There is no reason why the African in Africa should not be developed individually and socially as any other race in the world. The trouble is the African has not had enough contact with European Civilization. No doubt he has had too much contact with the evils of civilized nations, and too little contact with their virtues. Civilization, like learning, shows that " a little is a dangerous thing." Africans, like other peoples, must drink deep. How easy it is to copy vices! It is difficult to develop a civilization anywhere that really develops the individual as well as society at large. It will be more difficult in Africa, but the difficulty does not lessen the moral obligation of civilized powers toward Africa any more than it destroys the power of European Civilization to actualize for the African his highest social destiny.

THE MEDICINE-MAN AS A MORAL AGENT

The medicine-man is a prime factor in the equation of Vai morals. For the moral good or ill he is consulted in all important matters. When a child is born and the parents desire to know its fate or fortune they consult the

[3] "History of Civilization in Europe," Guizot, p. 13.

medicine-man, who claims to be able to tell them everything they wish to know. He demands his fee in advance, and sometimes he makes a lucky guess. More often he tells what proves to be untrue or puts in a condition which makes his prediction worthless. The medicine-man knows that he does not know and cannot foretell the future of an individual; he knows that he is encouraging superstition and taxing ignorance, and for his fee he continues to perpetrate what he knows to be a fraud. In all these cases his moral influence is not for good. If one individual desires to injure another he goes to the medicine-man to have him " witched." The medicine-man takes his fee with the understanding that he is to do certain work. Very often he does nothing, but in some cases he secures death by directly or indirectly administering poison. In these instances his moral influence is bad, because he encourages malice and revenge; but he reaches his lowest depths when he becomes a secret instrument for the commission of the foulest crimes. The medicine-man unquestionably often has an immoral influence, and he is always careful to secure his fee in advance.

But as bad as the medicine-man may seem and frequently is, yet he exerts some good and wholesome influences. For instance, in the case of theft, the belief which he has engendered that through his medicine he can detect the thief is a most effective deterrent from the commission of this crime. And because of this belief, and not because of any medicine, he is often able to pick out the thief through the aid of circumstances, and to render the greatest service to society and the state. As a result of his influence in these cases, his medicine hung up on a bush in a common rag causes many a thief to pass by what he might otherwise take without detection. In cases of the infidelity of a wife the loyalty of many a woman is maintained merely because of the belief that the medicine-man would be able to detect her infidelity by means of his medicine. He, therefore, is a strong influence not only against the infidelity of a wife but against all those evils and crimes that so often follow in its trail.

His medicine allays the fears of the warrior and nerves the arm of him that is sent out in the service of his sovereign and his state. His medicine soothes the savage breast and saves it from the pains and pangs of fright and fear. In many ways the medicine-man calms the troubled soul and gives peace to him who is besieged on every hand by wicked, invisible, and malignant spirits. He is a product of African conditions, he was created as the great support of native institutions; and, with all his faults, under present conditions he is indispensable to African life.

MORAL INFLUENCE OF THEIR RELIGION

We have been considering the medicine-man as a moral agent; we now come to the moral influence of Vai religion. We have seen that among the Vais there are two long established religions,— the pagan and the Islamic,[4] emanating from which there are two separate and distinct moral influences. As the pagan religion no doubt existed prior to the introduction of the Muhammudan faith and is a product of African conditions, its moral

[4] It is meant that two religious systems have native roots throughout the tribe. Christianity, in comparison with the others, just started yesterday. It has hardly had time to enter the heart of the tribe and manifest itself in all the varied phases of Vai life. Besides, many who accept Christianity go to Christian centers to live.

VAI CLOTH HAMMOCK AND BASKET

Facing Page 122

aspect is of special interest to the Negro race. The Vais are surrounded, like all West Africans, with a striking and abnormal physical environment. It has been so severe upon the pagans of to-day that they have been unable to throw off the religion which this abnormal environment imposed. One of the moral results of Vai paganism is that it encourages ignorance and superstition. Its tendency is to lessen the possibility of reforming itself or of being reformed.

The Vai paganism, with its beliefs in a multiplicity of invisible spirits malignant to men and capable of assuming varied forms, requires for its existence a comparatively low order of intellect. The intelligence is so low that the moral sense hardly rises above a form of egoism. Among the lowest of this class of Vais duty has little place in their moral conduct. They are so busy trying to protect themselves against imaginary and evil spirits that they have neither inclination nor time to consider the improvement of their moral code. It is cold, rigid, and selfish. The great motive which seems dominant is to secure some immediate physical good or to escape some immediate physical pain. The order of intellect of these pagans is not high enough to give much consideration, if any, to abstract ideas of right and wrong. The moral influence of the pagan religion, within its scope, is very great; that is to say, what their religious faith requires they sincerely do. The great misfortune is that the requirement is too small, material, and selfish.

I have called attention to what seem the bad influences of paganism among the Vais, but these bad influences themselves appear to have developed something for the good of the Negro. The greater portion of pagan life among the Vais is taken up with matters appealing to the religious side of their nature. The pagan Vai lives in a constant state of fear. His religion consists chiefly in making offerings and sacrifices to propitiate the anger of beings bent upon his ruin. In fact he is sacrificing so much that his life is a series of sacrifices, and he is sacrificing not to beings who command his love and devotion but to what seem to him wicked and sinister spirits, with designs upon his life and fortune. Long practice in making sacrifices under such circumstances is calculated to develop the capacity to endure great injury and hardship at the hand of another without entertaining the spirit of revenge. So that slowly the way is being paved for altruism in the very nature and character of the individual. The natural effect of pagan religion among the Vais is to give spiritual training in many of the following essentials of morals:

" To do good to others; to sacrifice for their benefit your own wishes; to love your neighbor as yourself; to forgive your enemies; to restrain your passions; to honor your parents; to respect those who are set over you; these, and a few others are the sole essentials of morals." [5]

The spiritual nature of the Negro has often excited comment. The meekness with which the American Negro endured the cruelties of slavery and his loyalty to the southern people during the rebellion have both been the subjects of comment. The latter has been cited to his credit and it may be that the former can be. The New Zealanders, the American Indians, the natives of the

[5] Introduction to " Civilization in England," by H. T. Buckle, p. 103, Robertson Edition.

Fiji and of the Sandwich Islands, before the civilization of the white man have passed or are passing from the stage of action. The American Negro alone seems to increase and develop. It may be that the Negro's life and training in West Africa have been of service to him in the United States of America.

The physical conditions among the Vais are no worse than they are elsewhere throughout West Africa. The fetich and amulet occupy a large place in native religious life in Africa as well as among Muhammudan tribes.[6]

The moral influences of Islam among the Vais is not so difficult to determine. The moral code of the Islamic Prophet is fashioned after the Sinaitic laws in two series, of five precepts each. These precepts are well known among the Vai Mussulmen. They might be named as follows:

" First, to acknowledge no other gods but God; second, to show respect to parents; third, not to kill children on account of dread of starvation; fourth, to preserve chastity; fifth, to protect the life of others except where justice demands the contrary; sixth, to keep inviolate the property of orphans; seventh, to employ just weights and measures; eighth, not to overburden slaves; ninth, judges to be impartial; tenth, to keep oaths sacred and the covenants with God." [7]

Such are the precepts which are taught by the priests of Islam among the Vais. Their moral influence has given

[6] Muhammudans make fetiches, amulets, and so on, consisting of pieces of paper containing words and lines from the Koran, which are worn by the Africans and which may be purchased for a fee.

[7] "The Races of Man," by Oscar Peschel, p. 303.

a higher tone to the life of the Muhammudan Vais than is to be found among the pagan Vais. But the fact that Islamic teachings do not disturb the institutions of polygamy and slavery prevents them from developing the kind of moral excellence that exists among Christian nations. However, the knowledge of the Koranic faith and moral code gives to the Muslim Vais a high order of individual intelligence and moral consciousness. It is seen in the dignity and importance which characterize the individual conduct of the Muhammudan adherents. It is noticed in all the institutions of the tribe. And in nothing is it so striking as in the abstinence from strong drink, gambling, and the common vices of the other Vai people. The scarcity of the means for disseminating the knowledge of the Koran prevents a wider diffusion of the moral principles that it teaches. So that while the moral standard is much higher among the Muslims than among the pagan Vais the degree of its excellence varies according to individual worth and the knowledge of Koranic morals.

THE MORAL INFLUENCE OF THEIR SOCIAL INSTITUTIONS

The moral life of the Vais is the product of their social institutions and their severe physical environments. These institutions grow out of the necessities of government for the tribe under circumstances which suggest and enforce their superstitions and beliefs. The beri and sande institutions prepare the young for the duties of native life, of the family, and of the state. They prepare them morally as well as intellectually. The young are trained to respect their parents and elders, to be loyal to the king, and to obey the laws,— all the essentials for family harmony are emphasized,— and they are not only instructed in the duties of the living to one another, according to native ideas, but they are taught to respect the dead.

But in the discharge of these duties to the family, the individual, the state, and the dead, as well as to the gods, temptations present themselves and bad habits and vices steal upon them before they are aware of the fact. For example, the various gatherings of the people for social pleasure and enjoyment afford opportunities for the beginning of many evils which lead to immorality and crime. At these meetings the native women dress according to their custom for participation in the dances and the promenades. Many of them are very attractive. These are also the times when the men display their wealth, attraction, and power. Young girls, given by their parents in marriage to men whom they do not love, often fall in love with other men. Sometimes they are attracted by the charms or wealth of men other than their husbands, and this means contentions and the breaking up of homes.

It is on such occasions that young men who gamble meet with those who do not, and often lead them by degrees to take up the gambling habit, with its temptations to steal, to lie, to fight, and to kill. It is at the social functions and dances that those who drink gin and rum carry it to excess and fasten upon others this liquor habit; thus they unbridle passion, deaden intellect, weaken and undermine character, and multiply all their misery and shame. So that while the aim and the effect of native institutions are to govern the individual in the home, in the state, and in society at large, and to develop in him a moral sense and the courage to live the native life according to native law, yet in some of these institutions

there are influences introduced that lessen and sometimes
even destroy the happiness of native life.

In many a Vai town I have availed myself of the opportunity to see both sides. I recall no instance more
striking than my experience at Boma. The king had just
died. Boma was crowded for a week with people from
the neighboring towns and half-towns. The feast was
spread. Everybody ate. The drinkers drank, the
singers sang, and there was music and the revelry of the
dance. But amid all the merriment and debauchery of
the town the Muhammudans went regularly five times
a day to their mosques to render homage and devotion
to their God. To lessen the evils of such an occasion
Islam has done a great deal for the Vais and no doubt
in the future will do more. As it was, many refused to
participate in the revelry and many turned away in disgust.

Mr. F. P. Noble, speaking of the morals of the Negro,
makes this startling statement, " The Negro is unmoral." [8]
Mr. Noble is the author of a most comprehensive survey
of African missions. His splendid effort is embodied
in two volumes, liberal in spirit and classic in literary
form. His disposition to do full justice to the Negro
renders important his reiteration of this old erroneous
indictment of the morals of the Negro race. It is strange
that so fair a writer should make so serious and sweeping
a statement against any member of the human family
without accompanying it with a proof of its truth. Yet
it is not so strange when we remember that until quite
recently competent travelers, scholars, scientists, and
ethnologists were unable to penetrate beyond the mere
surface of Negro life in Africa, on account of climatic

[8] " The Redemption of Africa," by F. P. Noble, Vol. I, p. 167.

difficulties, the variety of Negro languages and dialect, and the veil and mystery with which the Africans enshroud the inner elements of their lives and institutions. And notwithstanding the fact that the world for centuries placed a commercial premium on the proved actual, and potential inferiority of the Negro, no one has ever been able to do more than indulge in the statement of half truth and in the publication of wilful and wicked falsehoods against the race.

The time was when the charge that the Negro is an inferior creature would go unchallenged. The world then considered it in harmony with its economic interest. Its ignorance of the Negro was its bliss.[9] But the situation has materially changed.[10] Africa is practically divided among the nations of Europe. It is now to the best interest of the African colonizing powers to know the Negro as he really is, in order that they may govern him without friction and develop his country to the best advantage. The times demand knowledge and facts of the Negro in Africa. The great Powers are being impressed more and more with the necessity of knowing the truth. The great trend of the world's economic thought is to enforce this view.[11] It seems now that we will get the facts. The inner life of the Negro is being

[9] " I need say nothing more regarding Appendix I; it is a mine of knowledge concerning a highly developed set of natives of the true Negro stem, particularly valuable because, during recent years, we have been singularly badly off for information on the true Negro." From " West African Studies," by M. H. Kingsley, Preface, p. viii. This is especially true since Europe charged itself with the government of African peoples and races.

[10] " As to Leopard Spots," an open letter to Thomas Dixon, Jr., by Kelly Miller, pamphlet, 1905. This is one of the ablest defenses ever made to the attacks upon the Negro race, and should be read by every American citizen, white and black.

[11] Benjamin Kid, in the *Independent*, September 8, 1904.

studied and presented by competent minds, by men conversant with the dialects and languages of the localities that are being studied. Conclusions now regarding the Negro should be based on facts gleaned from observation made during a residence among the people by those who have mingled with Negroes in their own homes. People that think will hardly accept the theory now that "the Negro is unmoral," unless that theory be supported by the competent personal observation of the person expressing it or by facts pointed out by such high authorities as Miss M. H. Kingsley, Dr. Freeman, Dr. Nassau, Mr. T. J. Alldridge, Capt. C. B. Wallis, Mr. John Harford, Mr. Caseley Hayford, Mr. John Sarbah, Mr. E. D. Morel, M. le Comte de Cardi, and Sir A. B. Ellis. I have searched the works of these able authors in vain to find the facts that prove that "the Negro is unmoral."

On the other hand, the works of Dr. E. W. Blyden prove the morality of the race. The author of " Christianity, Islam, and the Negro Race," " From West Africa to Palestine," " The African Problem," " The African Society and Miss Mary H. Kingsley," and numerous articles concerning the African and his continent has presented facts enough to convince any mind not sealed against the truth that the Negro is not " unmoral." The fact is just as he says :

" There is no doubt that in spite of the countless books which have been published on Africa, there still exists in Europe [12] deplorable ignorance of the true character and condition of the natives, and not only among ' the men in the street,' but often among those who have become responsible for the government of large portions of this

[12] And in America also.

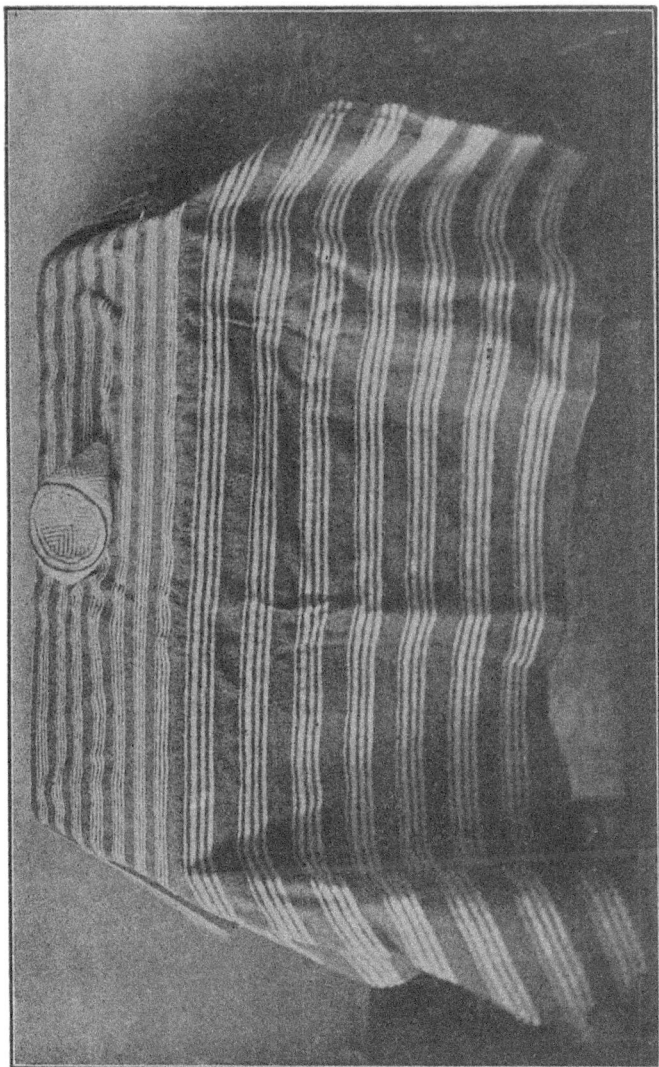

VAI CLOTH AND CAP

continent, since the so-called partition of Africa has taken place." [13]

To say that " the Negro is unmoral " is tantamount to saying that he has no moral perception,— that his life involves no idea whatever of morality.[14] In spite of the works of the previously named eminent authorities on the Negro and those of the 18th century and before, the inner life, past and present, of the great black race occupying a broad belt of territory across the African Continent from Senegal to the Red Sea for the most part is still unknown. But as far as it has been studied, the results disclosed will not warrant the conclusion that " the Negro is unmoral." But even if they did, the greater mass of the millions of African blacks, when studied and known, might reverse the conclusion. Basing her opinion on what was known at that time, Miss Kingsley said:

" If the Europeans only knew the African as he really is, they might say the African is very different from the European, yet would say he is a very fine fellow, and we can be friends." [15]

How many individuals of Occidental Civilization are there who have not confused difference with inferiority, and who are not still deceived by the thought that to be different from them and their civilization is to be inferior?[16] Few have suffered more from this error

[13] "The African Society and Miss Mary H. Kingsley," by Dr. E. W. Blyden, p. 7.
[14] See definition of unmoral, Webster's Unabridged.
[15] "The African Journal and Miss Mary H. Kingsley," by Dr. E. W Blyden, p. 7.
[16] " No one can have failed to observe how common it is for men

than has the Negro, but this delusion is being swept away by knowledge. This brings us to Miss Mary H. Kingsley.

This remarkable woman traveled extensively in West Africa. She wrote two splendid books: " The Travels in West Africa" and "The West African Studies." She possessed a phenomenal talent for studying the African. With subtle mental grasp she penetrated beneath the thin covering of deceitful appearance and empty forms, and touching the heart of Negro life, she felt the power and charm of his better and nobler self. She caught a glimpse of the Negro as he is, and returning from her vision alone she effectively pleaded his cause before a world ignorant of his ways. While on her last trip to Africa, and in her last letter to the press, she wrote:

" The white race seems to me to blame in saying that all the reason for its interference in Africa is the improvement of the native African, and then to start on altering institutions without in the least understanding them, and the African to blame for not placing clearly before the Anglo-Saxon what African institutions really are, and so combating the false and exaggerated view given of them by stray travelers, missionaries, and officials (who for their own aggrandisement exaggerate the difficulties and dangers with which they have to deal). It is mere human nature for them to do this thing, but the effect produced on the minds of our statesmen has terrible consequences."

to make their own tastes and excellencies the measure of all goodness, pronouncing all that is broadly different from them to be imperfect or low, or of a secondary value." " History of European Morals," by W. E. H. Lecky, Vol. I, p. 156.

Again and again she urges that there should be some organized method of studying the native laws and customs and publishing accounts of them, so that

"you who know European culture, and who also know African culture, will take your place as true ambassadors and peacemakers between the two races, and place before the English statesman the true African — destroy the fancy African made by exaggeration that he has now in his mind." [17]

Following the death of Miss Kingsley, and under the name of the African Society, a noble band of men and women have undertaken the consummation of the work which has been so ably begun. As Dr. Blyden says:

"Their concern is not with the physical or material, but with the psychological aspect of the question. They have organized themselves to set free the soul of their protégé from influences incompatible with his race individuality and race life; to show the. world — Africans helping in the work — that the African has a culture of his own — to explain that culture, and assist him to develop it." [18]

Associated with this movement, either actively or in their writings, are some of the most eminent persons before the English public. . I can mention only a few,— Lord Cromer, Sir George T. Goldie, the Count de Cardi, the Rt. Hon. John Morley, Sir Alfred Lyall, the Rt. Hon.

[17] "The African Journal and Miss Mary H. Kingsley," by Dr. E. W. Blyden, p. 7.
[18] "The African Journal and Miss Mary H. Kingsley," by Dr. E. W. Blyden, p. 7.

H. H. Asquith, Dr. J. Scott Keltie, Sir Matthew Nathan, H. D'Egville, Mr. George Macmillan, Sir Alfred Jones, Sir H. H. Johnston, and the Rt. Hon. Lord Avebury. Besides these persons and others prominent in England are some able West African Negro authors, such as the well known Dr. Blyden, Mr. Caseley Hayford,[19] and Mr. John Sarbah,[20] the author of "Fanti Customary Laws."

Before Miss Kingley published her "West African Studies" Sir A. B. Ellis, M. le Comte de Cardi, Mr. John Harford, Mr. John Sarbah, and a few others had already made valuable contributions to the study of the Negro in Africa. And since her death other important and instructive volumes have been added to the list: one by Dr. Nassau,[21] who has spent over half a century on the West Coast, living among the Bantu tribes and who was considered by Miss Kingsley as perhaps the ablest authority on the West Coast of Africa; and one by Mr. E. D. Morel, who, under the title of "Affairs of West Africa," gives to the public a rich fund of information about the Negro. A second edition of Mr. Sarbah's book has appeared, of which Mr. Morel wrote:

"'Fanti Customary Laws' has been universally regarded since the appearance of the first edition in 1897 as the only real standard work on the aboriginal jurisprudence of the Gold Coast people, and as one of the most valuable ethnological contributions extant of that people." [22]

[19] Author of "Institutions of the Gold Coast."
[20] Mr. John Sarbah is not a member of the African Society in London.
[21] "Fetichism in West Africa," by Dr. Robert Hamill Nassau.
[22] The *West African Mail*, August 12, 1904, p. 458.

This is high tribute, from high authority, to a native Negro of West Africa. Another very valuable volume has appeared,— the one by Mr. T. J. Alldridge on " Sherbro and its Hinterland." The writer of this book has passed thirty years in Africa and traveled over 6000 miles among its people. Still another volume has appeared under the title, " Advance of our West African Empire," by Capt. C. B. Wallis, now British Consul at Monrovia. Captain Wallis has had a rich and varied experience among the tribes on the West Coast, and his work is a valuable contribution to West African literature.

So if there ever was any justification for the statement that " the Negro is unmoral," it has now passed away in the light of a broader knowledge of the facts. The quotations from the authorities now extant on the Negro and his life showing that he has not only moral conceptions but moral standards would make a volume. I will venture to give one from Sir A. B. Ellis, whose works concerning the tribes of West Africa are regarded as models. In discussing one phase of morality among the Yoruba peoples, he says:

" At present, the feeling of annoyance which a Yoruba bridegroom experiences when he finds that his bride has been unchaste, is not due to jealousy or sentiment, but to a sense of injury, because his rights acquired by betrothal have been trespassed upon; but no doubt, in course of time, the sentimental grievance would be produced. Whether this feeling ever extends to the lowest classes is uncertain, but at all events it has scarcely done so in Europe." [23]

[23] " Yoruba-Speaking Peoples," by Sir A. B. Ellis, p. 184.

In quoting the above passage, I must say that I fully recognize that many things that are said by Sir Ellis in the chapter " Marriage Laws and Customs," at first glance may be thought to support the statement of Mr. Noble, but when they are thoroughly understood and carefully considered they will be found to prove that the Yoruba-Speaking Peoples are unquestionably possessed of moral conceptions and standards. And the whole chapter, so far as these peoples are concerned, contains a most splendid refutation of the absurd idea that " the Negro is unmoral." Sir Ellis says that marriage is prohibited by the Yorubas between all relations closer than second cousins; that for the first reported neglect of delinquent husbands a palaver is held by the wife's family; and for subsequent offences the wife may leave, and in some cases her family may flog the offending husband. Adultery is punishable by divorce or death, but may be settled by damages. It is hardly necessary to cite other facts from this author showing the morals of the Negro in the light of the following statement from a high authority on ethical subjects:

" If then incest is prohibited, and community of wives replaced by ordinary polygamy, a moral improvement will have been effected, and a standard of virtue formed. But this standard soon becomes the starting point of new progress." [24]

Sir James Macintosh, speaking on the universal character of moral foundations, remarks:

" The facts which lead to the formation of moral rules

[24] " History of European Morals," Vol. I, p. 103, by W. E. H. Lecky.

are as accessible, and must be as obvious, to the simplest barbarian as to the most enlightened philosopher." [25]

The Negro might rest his case with the weight of reason as well as of scholarship in favor of the universal existence of the innate moral faculty in the human race. But tried by the ultimate ethical sanctions now generally recognized by both the utilitarian and intuitive schools,[26] the Negro has all the essentials of morals, and where unmodified by the baneful effects of outside evil influences, the great mass in Africa, according to their own standard established by their own institutions, live a moral life. They have their physical, political, social, natural,[27] and religious sanctions, operating among them under the severity of African conditions, and supplying all the motives for their moral lives. The Negro tribe that has no moral conceptions is yet to be discovered and described. Of the dozen or more in Liberia none are so low but what they have "Greegree Bushes" or institutions for the special instruction and protection of their girls; laws regulating marriage and defining crime, and numerous customs the purpose of which is to secure respect for the aged, obedience to parents, reverence for the fetich gods, and to save the captured in war from the pangs of death. As far as disclosed by competent students, similar conditions exist among all the pagan tribes. You may judge of the morals of the millions of the finer Ne-

[25] "Life of Mackintosh," Vol. I, pp. 119-122, by his son, 1835.
[26] "Principles of Morals and Legislation," Chap. II, p. 28, Bentham; "History of European Morals," Vol. I, p. 22, by W. E. H. Lecky.
[27] Called natural because arising from the nature of humanity to sympathize. See Mill's "Dissertations," Vol. I, p. 137.

groes of the Sudan, of whom, in speaking of Timbuctu, Lady Lugard wrote:

" Here the learned of Spain and Morocco and Arabia were proud to come and share the wisdom of the natives of the Sudan, and long biographical lists have been preserved of the distinguished professors, black and white, who taught in the schools of this and other towns, or enriched different departments of science, art, and literature with their labors." [28]

[28] " Journal of the Royal Colonial Institute," by Lady Lugard.

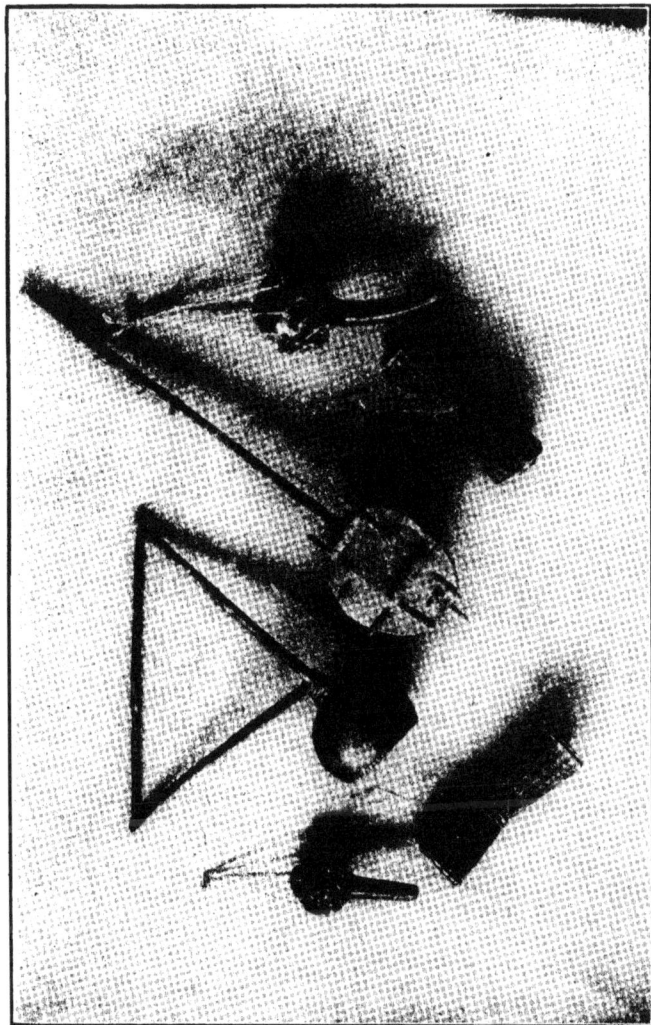

SOME VAI MUSICAL INSTRUMENTS

Facing Page 138

SPECIMENS OF VAI LITERATURE

PHONETIC CHART OF THE
VAI CHARACTERS

Phonetic Chart of the Vei Characters.

Vei	Eng.	Vei	Eng.	Vei	Eng.	Vei	Eng.	Vei	Eng.
⟨⟩	ā	⟨⟩	gā	⟨⟩	lā	⟨⟩	rā	⟨⟩	wā
⟨⟩	e	⟨⟩	gē	⟨⟩	lē	⟨⟩	rē	⟨⟩	wē
⟨⟩	i	⟨⟩	gā	⟨⟩	lā	⟨⟩	rā	⟨⟩	wā
⟨⟩	o	⟨⟩	gō	⟨⟩	lō	⟨⟩	rō	⟨⟩	wē
⟨⟩	u	⟨⟩	gū	⟨⟩	lū	⟨⟩	rū	⟨⟩	wŭ
⟨⟩	ŏ	⟨⟩	gŏ	⟨⟩	lŏ	⟨⟩	rŏ	⟨⟩	wŏ
⟨⟩	ĕ	⟨⟩	gĕ	⟨⟩	lĕ	⟨⟩	rĕ	⟨⟩	wĕ
⟨⟩	bā	⟨⟩	lā	⟨⟩	mā	⟨⟩	sā	⟨⟩	yā
⟨⟩	bē	⟨⟩	lē	⟨⟩	mē	⟨⟩	sē	⟨⟩	yē
⟨⟩	bā	⟨⟩	lā	⟨⟩	mā	⟨⟩	sā	⟨⟩	yā
⟨⟩	bō	⟨⟩	lō	⟨⟩	mō	⟨⟩	sō	⟨⟩	yō
⟨⟩	bū	⟨⟩	hū	⟨⟩	mą	⟨⟩	sū	⟨⟩	yŭ
⟨⟩	bŏ	⟨⟩	hŏ	⟨⟩	mŏ	⟨⟩	sŏ	⟨⟩	yŏ
⟨⟩	bĕ	⟨⟩	hĕ	⟨⟩	mĕ	⟨⟩	sĕ	⟨⟩	yŏ
⟨⟩	dā	⟨⟩	jā	⟨⟩	nā	⟨⟩	tā	⟨⟩	xā
⟨⟩	dē	⟨⟩	jē	⟨⟩	nē	⟨⟩	tē	⟨⟩	xē
⟨⟩	dā	⟨⟩	jā	⟨⟩	nā	⟨⟩	tā	⟨⟩	xā
⟨⟩	dū	⟨⟩	jū	⟨⟩	nō	⟨⟩	tō	⟨⟩	xō
⟨⟩	ăŏ	⟨⟩	jŏ	⟨⟩	nū	⟨⟩	tū	⟨⟩	xū
⟨⟩	ăĕ	⟨⟩	jĕ	⟨⟩	nō	⟨⟩	tō	⟨⟩	xŏ
⟨⟩		⟨⟩		⟨⟩	nĕ	⟨⟩	tĕ	⟨⟩	xĕ
⟨⟩	fā	⟨⟩	kā	⟨⟩	pā	⟨⟩	vā		
⟨⟩	fē	⟨⟩	kē	⟨⟩	pē	⟨⟩	vē		
⟨⟩	fă	⟨⟩	kō	⟨⟩	pă	⟨⟩	vă		
⟨⟩	fō	⟨⟩	kŭ	⟨⟩	pō	⟨⟩	vō		
⟨⟩	tū	⟨⟩	kŏ	⟨⟩	pŭ	⟨⟩	vū		
⟨⟩	fŏ	⟨⟩	kŏ	⟨⟩	pŏ	⟨⟩	vŏ		

Double & Triple Consonants.

Vei	Eng	Vei	Eng	Vei	Eng	Vei	Eng	Vei	Eng
	chā		kpā		ndā		nyā		zhā
	chē		kpē		ndē		njē		zhē
	chä		kpä		ndä		mä		zhä
	chō		kpō		ndō		nyō		zhō
	chu		kpu		ndū		nyŭ		zhū
	chŏ		kpŏ		ndŏ		njŏ		zhŏ
	chě		kpě		ndě		nvě		zhě
	dhā		lhā		ngā		shō		**Miscellaneous**
	dhē		lhē		ngē		shē		ähn
	dhä		lbä		ngä		shä		fää
	Jhō		lbō		ngō		shō		hn
	Jhū		lbū		ngū		shū		kpnä
	Jhŏ		lbŏ		ngŏ		shŏ		nwä
	dhě		lhě		npě		shě		nwě
	gbā		ldā		njā		thā		whě
	gbē		ldō		njē		thō		
	gbä		ldä		njä		thä		
	gbu		ldū		njō		thō		**Punctuation Signs**
	gbŏ		ldŏ		njŏ		thŭ		bridge
	gbě		ldě		njě		thō		comma
			mbā		nkpā		whā		interrogation
	hnē		mbē		nkpē		whō		period
	hnä		mbä		nkpä		whä		exclamation
			mbō		nkpō				accent
	hnū		mbū		nkpū				detraction
	hnō		mbŏ		nkpŏ		whō		nunnation
	hně		mbě		nkpě		whě		continuation of sound

Compiled by Momolu Massaquoi Prince of Gallinas

VAI PROVERBS

CHAPTER VIII

VAI PROVERBS

(1)

"NO matter how poor an elephant is he cannot cross the bridge." When some one comes to the king to beg of him when times are a little hard with him he very often says that he is poor himself, but he gives the man something, adding, "No matter how poor an elephant is he cannot cross the bridge,"— meaning that no matter how poor the king may be he cannot allow the man to go without having given him something.

(2)

"The monkey wants to get honey, but he has no ax to cut the tree." When a poor king is ambitious to build up his town and often remarks what he would do if he only had the money, he is reminded by somebody that "The monkey wants to get honey, but he has no ax to cut the tree."

(3)

"Black skillet is no good for making soup," or "Making soup in a black skillet is trouble." When they see a man doing something that it is thought will lead to trouble they ask the man, "Are you making soup in a black skillet?" It is the general opinion that soup cannot be made in a black skillet without trouble in that it all gets black, or else the person is so poor that he cannot afford to buy a pot.

(4)

" A baboon does not like cola for anything." A baboon was very hungry, and although he was accustomed to eat cola he slept under a cola tree all night, yet he complained of being hungry with cola nuts all about. Sometimes a person asks for something which he thinks he has lost but which is close at hand, 'perhaps in his pocket; when he finds it he says to himself, " A baboon does not like cola for anything."

(5)

" The pig drinks liquor, but the goat gets drunk." A slave boy raised in a rich family imagines that he can do just as he pleases,— in fact, he ventures to do things that his master would not do. Sometimes when he is doing some of these things he is sure to be told, " The pig drinks liquor, but the goat gets drunk."

(6)

" We catch a catfish because he does not like straw." The catfish when he sees straw in the water begins to fight it, and thus is often baited by it, or, the catfish does not like straw, and that is what makes him come to land. If a man is an enemy to another man and is always working up stories against him, one day instead of the stories injuring the enemy it falls upon the witness, and the people repeat to him the proverb, " The catfish does not like straw, that is why he comes to land."

(7)

" A frightened man will say ' How d'ye do' to a leopard." When two men who have been enemies are

VAI GRASS WORK IN CAPS AND BAGS

Facing Page 148

forced into a contest in which they are both on the same side they are often twitted by those who knew of the former enmity by the proverb, " A frightened man will say ' How d'ye do ' to a leopard." The leopard is considered a very unfriendly creature in Africa.

(8)

" If a man raises a snake he must tie it." When a man has a bad boy or daughter who is always getting into trouble and he is called on to pay until a time comes when he declines to pay, somebody is sure to urge him to do so by quoting the words, " If a man raises a snake he must tie it."

(9)

" The cow follows the man that has salt." When a man is obliged to seek the favor of a rich man and often does things for nothing in order to get pay for a small job, the question is asked why is he always at the rich man's house. The answer is, " The cow follows the man who has salt."

(10)

" If one man eats beans he makes much straw." When two men have something and it is divided in each other's presence they are both contented. But if one of them is absent the likelihood of his being dissatisfied with the division is very great. In case the division made in the absence of one man happens to be fair and the man who was absent complains when he returns, his complaint is answered with, " If one man eats beans he makes much straw." In the case of beans, the absent man would refer on returning to the great quantity of hulls as evidence of the fact that much beans had been eaten.

(11)

"A little rain every day will make the rivers swell." People are encouraged to save money by repeating to them this old saying, which is used with respect to all matters that may be accomplished little by little or gradually.

(12)

The frog says, "I have nothing, but I have my hop." When a man is poor yet has something that no one else has in the country he is very proud of it,— for example, medicine. And when persons come to buy often may be heard repeating to himself, "I have nothing, but I have my hop."

(13)

"A man who waits on a monkey in a tree has shot it." A man goes to another man's house who has gone away and has not indicated when he will return. The stranger decides to wait until the man's return, and stays at his house. After a few hours or a day or so some of the family asks the man for what he is waiting. He replies that he is waiting for the return of the man of the house. He is asked if he was told when he would return and he says, " No." Then you may expect to hear, " A man who waits on a monkey in a tree has shot it."

(14)

"If the stomach is full, it is palaver; and if hungry, it is palaver." A poor man visits one man and is well

entertained, and returns home without having made any
"dash" for his entertainment. The host of the poor
man visits his town, and the poor man is unable to entertain him as he was entertained, but he desires to do
something, so he catches a chicken and takes it to the
good and kind visitor and presenting it conveys to the
visitor an idea of his situation when he repeats: "If the
stomach is full, it is palaver; and if hungry, it is palaver." So that hungry or otherwise, it is palaver for
the poor man.

(15)

"If I do not go in I must go by." When a native
vendor is carrying about his wares sometimes some person will see something he wants and takes it, but he
wishes to pay at another time. The vendor is almost
sure to refuse credit, and for this purpose it is very con-
venient to have a proverb: "If I do not go in, I must
go by."

(16)

"If I do not go to the Greegree Bush, you must send
my cloth." Every person that goes to the greegree bush
has her cloth taken from her. If she is finally rejected
from the bush, when she leaves she is entitled to have
her cloth back. It is the custom in having a big dinner
and dance for a number of people to put in their contributions in advance. Those who have so contributed are
entitled to the privileges of the dance. Sometimes a person who has so contributed is denied participation at the
dinner by mistake,— a mistake that arises from varying
causes in management, as, for instance, when the person
who admits the people is unacquainted with all who are

entitled to enter. When some one is thus rejected who is entitled to enjoy the privileges of the dinner he is sure to shout out, " If I do not go to the Greegree Bush, you must send my cloth."

(17)

" Hens never promise to give the chickens milk." A rich man very often will promise a poor man to help him, and when he helps the poor man in a way that is proper according to his judgment the poor man will still remain dissatisfied, and ask the rich man for something that he does not wish to give. When the poor man thus insists he is very likely to hear that " Hens never promise to give the chickens milk."

(18)

" If you cannot mend the gourd, how can you fix the bowl? " This saying is often applied to cobblers. For example, a goldsmith representing himself to be able to do all kinds of work, induces a man to give him an important job, but before he enters upon it his customer gives him a small article that he wishes mended. The smith, unable to repair the article, botches the work, yet he wants to undertake the much more important job. The deceived patron answers, " If you cannot mend the gourd how can you fix the bowl? "

(19)

" Why should a naked man fight for soap? " Soap is in great demand among the natives who wear clothes, and sometimes many of them contend over a single piece, but the naked man is seldom if ever seen to trouble himself about it. In native war a strange man in a town attacked is not expected to fight. If the town should be captured he would be set at liberty upon making known the fact that he was a stranger. But if a stranger should violate the custom and join the town people in resistance and should get killed, people who express their sorrow for him are likely to hear somebody ask, "Why should a naked man fight for soap?"

(20)

"The dog goes to the blacksmith shop for its bell, but what does the cat go for?" The officers and persons who are known to have business with the king may call upon him and remain for hours, and no comments upon their doing so will be made. But if persons whose business are not known,— or whom some people envy because of their favor with the king,— are seen to visit the king too often or to remain what is considered too long, somebody will comment upon it by saying, "The dog goes to the blacksmith shop for its bell, but what does the cat go for?"

(21)

"Man likes a full spoon but not an empty plate." A man who has been rich but who has squandered his money and become an object of pity excites the comment of those who knew him in his better days; and as he passes along the thoroughfare they often mutter to themselves, "Man likes a full spoon but not an empty plate."

(22)

"The man left the other man in one field," or, "The lazy man is always left behind." A man has a son attending school. Every now and then the son finds some excuse to stay out of school, until the father, alarmed, begins to scold, when he is almost sure to say, "The man left the other man in one field," which is to say that two men set out to go to a town, but one of the men trifling along the way was left in one old field.

(23)

"My spear has gone through the banana tree." The banana tree is regarded by the African as a very valuable tree, and it contributes a great deal to his support. No one would knowingly do anything to injure or kill the banana tree. Information reaches the king that a terrible crime has been committed, and very strict orders are issued for the capture of the malefactors. When they are caught and brought before the king he is surprised to find that they are his own kinsmen. He conveys to all the full depth of his sorrow when to himself he sadly repeats, "My spear has gone through the banana tree."

(24)

"If crazy men are in the country, it is not difficult to find slaves." The finer tribes of West Africa believe that one way to get rich is to get a plenty of slaves. They also believe that any person who would consent to be a slave is not possessed of full mental power. A Vai trader had a clerk who was constantly making mistakes, sometimes by giving too much change, and sometimes by selling too cheaply, and in speaking of this clerk a Vai man used this expression, "If crazy men are in the country, it is not difficult to find slaves."

(25)

" The poor man raises children for the rich." Among
the Africans the poor man does not himself consume any
very fine commodity that he may raise, but sells it to
some rich man. Their children, however, are their most
precious jewels. When a poor man, carrying his fine
rooster, goat, or cow to a rich man, is asked why he does
not keep it and eat it himself, his only answer is the
proverb, " The poor man raises children for the rich,"
and therefore such small things as fowls, goats, and
cows must necessarily belong to the rich, too.

(26)

" The chicken without feathers says, ' The chicken with
feathers gets cold; why do you ask me why I am cold?' "
When there is a scarcity of food articles and men of
means are unable to buy what they want the friends of
a poor man sometimes joke him about the scarcity of his
food, and he finds some relief in the old saying: " The
chicken without feathers says, ' The chicken with feathers gets cold; why do you ask me why I am cold?' "

(27)

" The country devil when he has good dress plays in
the daytime." The country devil plays at night when
she has not good dress so that she may not be detected
and recognized. Her continued influence depends upon
the concealment of her identity, and although she is
dressed as a man she is nevertheless a woman. The
Vai man goes off and makes money and comes home
and gives a big dinner in display. He has never given
a dinner before. Among the many persons invited to

dine will be some to ask, " Why did this man give this big dinner? " and there will be some to answer, " The country devil when he has good dress plays in the day-time."

(28)

" The person who has not dropped anything will look for it with his foot." A Vai man, with two or three brothers, gets into trouble and must pay a large sum of money. The brothers of the man in trouble go about the town telling the people that they have trouble because their brother has to pay a big sum of money. Later these brothers are seen spreeing away their means, and some one will ask them, " How can you spend your money so when your brother is in trouble? " The brother who is really in trouble remarks, " The person who has not dropped anything will look for it with his foot."

(29)

" The chicken that wastes the palm-oil his leg will be red." In a family where there are several brothers one of them is thought to have committed a theft. The accusers in their zeal to catch the guilty are willing to punish all the brothers when some old head will object on the ground that " The chicken that wastes the palm-oil his leg will be red," and will insist on ferreting out the guilty from the innocent.

(30)

" The man who did not attend the funeral says the dead man had plenty of witch." It is customary among the Vais to examine the dead for a witch by what we would consider a post-mortem examination. Sometimes they find evidences of no witch, at other times of a small witch, and again of a big witch. When evidence of a small witch is found persons who were not present will circulate reports of the finding of a big witch, illustrating the nature of man to exaggerate. So that when any Vai man begins to tell anything that seems unreasonable, so much so as to be tantamount to a falsehood, the unbelieving quote the proverb, " The man who did not attend the funeral says the dead man had plenty of witch."

(31)

"The paddle you find in the canoe is the paddle that will carry you across." It is a custom among the Vais to send up the country to the King's for slaves; nearly all the time the King has some person or persons imprisoned in sticks to be sold as slaves. Upon application for slaves the King usually sells only those who are in sticks. If the slave-buyers insist on getting more it is pointed out that " The paddle you find in the canoe is the paddle that will carry you across."

(32)

" In the absence of the leopard the bush cat is King of the bush." Sometimes the King visits a neighboring town for a short time. During his absence some people are almost sure to take advantage of the situation and do some wrong. Sometimes in a general spree some persons will get drunk and rage in row and riot, or some ambitious man whom the King has authorized to keep a lookout until his return abuses his authority and by his acts of injustice arouses just indignation, some of the old reliable people of the town may be seen talking to themselves or to others, during the course of which they will often repeat, " In the absence of the leopard the bush cat is King of the bush."

(33)

" One bad goat will spoil the herd." There is one man who is buying palm-oil in a town. One dishonest man mixes water with his palm-oil and sells it. The man who bought the palm-oil and water gets vexed and refuses to buy any more palm-oil because of this fraud having been practiced upon him. Those who have been honest in making and selling palm-oil and must suffer for another's wrong are reminded that " One bad goat will spoil the herd."

(34)

" The wise man is father of the fool." A rich or intelligent man in Africa is considered a big man, and very often such a man has a bad son or daughter who seems to have none of the attributes of the family and whose conduct repeatedly reflects upon the family name. Sometimes the son will get into trouble as fast as his father gets him out, or the daughter will take up a life of shame and her acts will furnish themes for social gossip. It is under these sad circumstances that we hear, " The wise man is father of the fool."

(35)

" A boil comes on the leg of the small bird." It is a belief that a boil comes on the leg of a small bird because of the difficulty of treating his small and frail limb and that on a large bird they can easily be pre-

VAI DRESS, FARM AND WAR HATS

Facing Page 158

vented. When a poor man gets into trouble and is unable to pay and must remain in a native prison he is compared to the little bird with a boil on his limb. If he had the money he could pay and thus, like a big bird's being saved from having a boil, he could avoid imprisonment. So when a man is seen in sticks some passer-by will remark, " A boil comes on the leg of a small bird."

(36)

" The lame man complains of the head of his carrier." A person is in poor circumstances, and in a time of distress a sympathizer and friend takes him in and gives him shelter and food. After a little while the person taken in begins to complain of his food or some inconvenience he has to suffer. When the complaints reach the ears of his friend the Vai man says, " The lame man complains of the head of his carrier."

(37)

" Mushroom in a bugabug hill does not know that the other mushroom has run." Mushrooms are usually found in the Vai country one on one side of the bugabug hill and one on the other side. When one comes out on one side frequently the one on the other side has disappeared. One man gets into trouble and is placed in sticks, and he sends a messenger to his brother or friend to inform him of his trouble. When the messenger arrives he finds in prison the brother or friend, who says to the messenger, " Mushroom in a bugabug hill does not know that the other mushroom has run."

(38)

" Small palm-nuts are not slaves for the large one."

A free-born boy while playing gets into a fight with the King's son. The neighbors gather, and some of them tell the little free-born boy that he should not be fighting with the King's son. In the meantime the father of the little boy appears and overhears the admonition given to his son, and he resents it by saying, " Small palm-nuts are not slaves for the large ones."

(39)

" It is better for a hungry man to go to the owner in the house than to the cook in the kitchen." When the people want to borrow or to buy something on credit sometimes a clerk will pretend that he owns the goods or has power to dispose of them on his own terms to enhance his own personal importance, but he continues to put the people off without disclosing the real owner or his limited authority. Then some of the disappointed will begin to talk about their disappointment, and some one will remind them that " It is better for a hungry man to go to the owner in the house than to the cook in the kitchen."

(40)

" If the man who tends the farm is rich, what must the owner be? " Very often a man who works for another through thrift and economy accumulates considerable property. A stranger in passing by with a person who belongs in the community admires the wealth of the workman and is told that he is only a servant or clerk for another man, when the stranger exclaims, " If the man who tends the farm is rich, what must the owner be? "

(41)

"You do not tell the rice-cutter that he has some rice before him." Sometimes a man will give to another a job of work to do and before the workman has completed it the employer, afraid that it will not be done well, points out in advance, before the workman has turned the work over, certain parts which have not been done, and a favorite retort of the workman is, "You do not tell the rice-cutter that he has some rice before him."

(42)

"A snake can run but he cannot outrun his head." Sometimes a strong young man takes a pride in fighting, and after a few combats is acknowledged as the champion of his neighborhood or his town. One day this young man begins a fight, and a big man in the community, hearing of it, starts out to stop him and to put the young fighter in his proper place. On the way the big man meets one who has been cowed by the strength and valor of the young fighter, and he advises the big man that it is no use for him to go, as he will not be able to conquer the young man. But if the big man is not deterred by these warnings and predictions, it is only necessary for him to say, "A snake can run, but he cannot outrun his head."

(43)

"The man who swims thinks that no one sees his feet." A thief steals something. When the people begin to investigate they find the evidences pointing to one man. They approach him and begin to question

him on the subject and to refer to some of the things
that point to him, in the thought, perhaps, that he might
confess; but the thief stoutly maintains his innocence,
and that so strongly that the people leave him, but they
leave with the thief this wise saying, " The man who
swims thinks that no one sees his feet."

(44)

" Your food is close to your stomach, but you must
put it in your mouth first." Sometimes among the Vais
a son or a nephew will take or desire to take the property of his father or uncle without waiting for the ordinary process of Vai custom. The son or nephew as
soon as his father or uncle dies proceéds to take what
he wants, since it all belongs to him, and he does not
quite see the necessity of complying with the custom of
carrying everything to the King first. His attention will
be called to the irregularity, and perhaps in the conversation some one will re-enforce his remarks by the
proverb, " Your food is close to your stomach, but you
must put it in your mouth first."

(45)

" No matter how bright the moon shines it is dark
in some places." The Vais educate their children, teaching them the Vai script as well as the Arabic, together
with the principles of knowledge from an African's
standpoint as well as the culture of the Koran and the
Arabs. Sometimes the people in a community exert themselves to put every child under the influence of education,
but in spite of all their efforts and success in educating
him some boy is sure to turn out badly. Then the old

people shake their heads and say, " No matter how bright the moon shines it is dark in some places."

(46)·

" When you meet two old ladies together, one is always older than the other." It is common among Africans to comment on one's wealth. A number of young men get together and during the course of the conversation one of them refers to a rich man he knows; another mentions one whom he claims has greater wealth; finally they reach two of whom they are unable to decide which has the greater wealth, and so they agree to take the matter to an old man, who will remind them of the wisdom of the fathers, " When you meet two old ladies together, one is always older than the other."

(47)

" No matter how long a dry leaf remains on the tree sometime it will fall down." The Vais in their large towns have their markets. Sometimes a man is able to secure credit from one of the traders but because he cannot pay he will stop coming to the market. He remains away so long that the trader begins to complain of his not coming, and before he complains long he will find some one who knows the old saying, " No matter how long a dry leaf remains on the tree sometime it will fall down."

(48)

" If you put a stick in a hole it will fool you, but not so with the hand." The Vais are a very intelligent people, and they like to have slaves wait upon them. When a bad slave is sent to do something and fails to do it, it is certain to furnish a subject for comment afterward among the neighbors. The master puts the blame on the slave, but somebody will transfer it to him saying, "If you put a stick in a hole it will fool you, but not so with the hand," implying that the master should have attended to the matter in person.

(49)

"No matter how much sense, the little boy will get the young cola from the tree." When a Vai man has a very bright boy he trusts him to do little things. He often sends him to market. No matter how satisfactorily the little boy performs this service the day he makes a mistake the father will reprove him, saying, "No matter how much sense, the little boy will get the young cola from the tree." The little boys are sent up the cola trees for colas, and the young colas are not good to eat.

(50)

"When a little boy slips off and goes into the tree and cannot get down he calls for his parents." War breaks out between two tribes, a third tribe declares neutrality, then the King warns all his subjects against taking any part in the war. One of his subjects joins the war in spite of warning, and is captured by the other side. He sends word to his King who declines to have anything to do with him; but the erring man's friends and relatives beg and entreat the King to take up the matter, and they clinch their appeal with the well-known saying: "When a little boy slips off and goes into the tree and cannot get down he calls for his parents,"—a strong plea to the parent feeling.

(51)

" When a small bird says ' I am fat ' you make a hole
in a little pot and reply, ' If your fat will fill this pot
then you are fat.' " In some of the Vai towns there is
a man who is always getting into trouble, but he seems
to get out every time. One day he gets into trouble from
which no one believes he will be able to escape. As it
is impossible to fill a pot with a hole in it, they say,
" When a small bird says ' I am fat ' you make a hole in
a little pot and reply, ' If your fat will fill this pot then
you are fat,' " which is expressive of their belief in the
impossibility of the man's being able to secure his re-
lease, and as much as to say, " If you get out of this
trouble, you are smart indeed."

(52)

" If you have not carried the war, you must not play
fight." When a man has a case and the native lawyer
who has promised to appear on the day set for trial for
him does not appear the man is sure to complain of this
action of the lawyer, which is condemned by the words,
" If you have not carried the war, you must not play
fight."

(53)

" If you have no one to carry the goat, do not let
it go into the mud." If the goat goes into the mud and
the owner has no one to carry it and he is obliged to
carry it across some place he is sure to get his clothes
dirty. A man's son gets into trouble, and the injured
party appeals early to the father in the matter, so that
the difficulty may be settled without much cost to the

father. But the father declines to have anything to do with it. Fearing that he will be obliged to take it up later when the trouble will be greater, the old saying is brought into service, "If you have no one to carry the goat, do not let it go into the mud."

(54)

"You always say a leopard's hide in speaking of its skin." When a man is King with much wealth sometimes through some misfortune or difficulty he suddenly becomes poor. The African looks down upon a poor man. Some of the people are likely in fun or in earnest to remind the King of his former wealth and his present poverty. His reply is likely to be, "You always say a leopard's hide in speaking of its skin."

(55)

"A shame man cannot eat crawfish." The people like crawfish, but if they eat it they make noise in cracking the encasing and the neighbors will call for some, hence they say, "A shame man cannot eat crawfish." Sometimes a man has another man arrested for some offense, but the arrested man, by his own talk or the influence and talk of his friends, frightens the person who had him arrested so that the prosecution halts and wavers. The prosecutor is advised to drop the matter, and although he does not carry forward his case he declines to dismiss it and recites the story of the crime or offense. After a time some one, observing that the man is afraid to do anything, expresses his disgust in this way, "A shame man cannot eat crawfish."

(56)

" Bugabug-hill says, ' If you do not want people to mash you, do not let the mushroom come.' " Some people like many friends and have many visitors, and some of them are sure to give trouble. So a friend or a member of your family will advise you against having so many friends, and they will give as their authority, " Bugabug hill says, ' If you do not want people to mash you, do not let the mushroom come.' "

(57)

" If a frizzled chicken lives in a town, the town cannot burn." Among the Vais to eat a frizzled chicken is good luck. Among the Vais there are some men who devote their time to peacemaking. When two men quarrel they go to them and stop it. If war is about to break out, they take up the causes with both sides in the interest of peace. In every difficulty their good influences and offices are felt for good. They are regarded as a blessing to any community. And so they live in those wise sayings that are handed down from generation to generation, " If a frizzled chicken lives in a town, the town cannot burn.'

(58)

" No man leaves the doctor's work for nothing." The Zo is the head of the Greegree Bush, an institution for the training of young Vai girls. The Zo is at the head of a great many things, and one of the departments under her is medicine. It is a position of great authority and influence. Besides being a good singer, one must belong to a family of money or power, for at the death

of the Zo two slave money (about six pounds sterling)
is to be paid by the family of the deceased to the King,
or the Zo cannot be buried. On the one hand people
are attracted by the prominence and importance of the
position, and on the other they are repelled by its grave
responsibilities. When it is refused it is for good and
fundamental reasons. When a man hires one man to
do a piece of work and he goes off without finishing
it sometime this workman meets his former employer and
is asked why he did not do the work; being ashamed to
give the reason he says that there was none. The employer insists to the contrary, for " No man leaves the
doctor's work for nothing."

(59)

" An old hen cannot turn the town for nothing." A
hen that will not attend to her chickens or hatch her
eggs is likely to be sold from one person to another until
she is sold around the town. So that when you see a
hen that has gone the round something is wrong with
her. A man brings you a good-looking boy and you
buy him. Later you ascertain that the boy steals. The
Vai man in commenting on the boy is sure to bring up
that " An old hen cannot turn the town for nothing."

(60)

" If a billy goat has his jewelry twenty years with the
silver smith, how many more years has he to dress? "
The billy goat has whiskers and some people put little
bags around his neck. The billy goat could hardly live
anything like twenty years. His day for dressing is
short. When you take your goods to the Vai tailor to
be made and every time you call he has not commenced

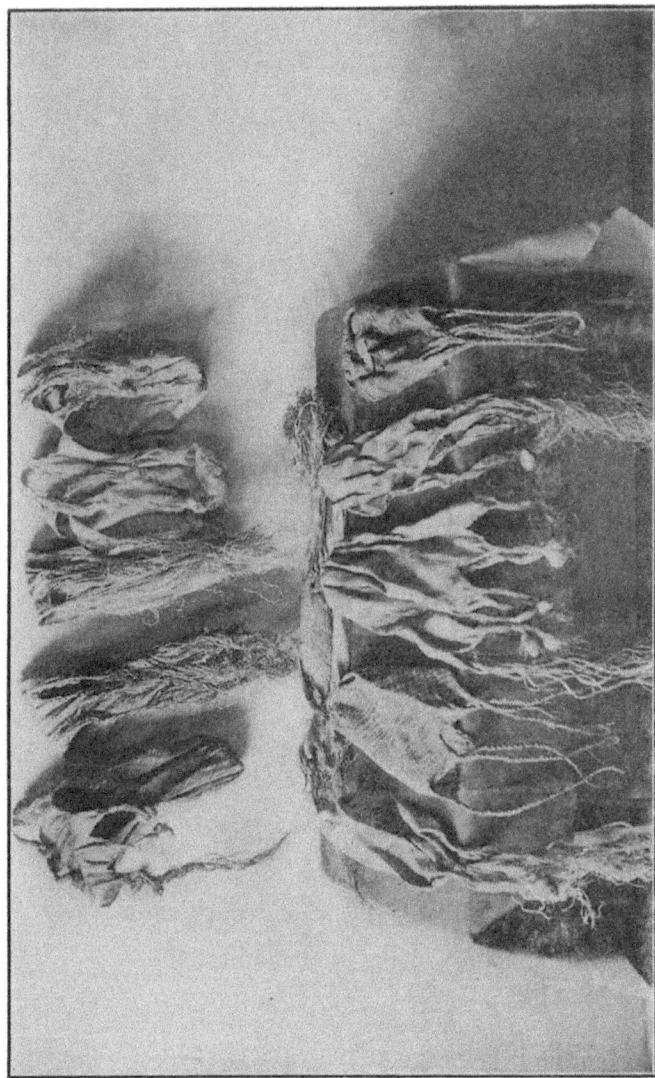

VAI GRASS WORK IN HANDBAGS

Facing Page 168

the work but promises and puts you off you are sure
to get tired after many postponements, and you indig-
nantly ask, " If a billy goat has his jewelry twenty years
with the silver smith, how many more years has he to
dress? "

(61)

" If you do not know two, look at the goat's head."
The goat has two horns, as everybody knows. Whenever a Vai man wants to insinuate that you do not possess ordinary sense,— as when he is trying to explain
to you something very plain to himself, something that
you cannot see nor understand,— he dismisses the matter in contempt, by saying, " If you do not know two,
look at the goat's head."

(62)

" The grippa feeds itself upon its own little fish."
Some poor Vai men have a number of boys in the family, such as nephews, cousins, etc. Every now and then
he sells one to some rich man. Some of his own relatives do not like this selling of the family, and finally
a protest is made. The explanation is that the boys
are to be redeemed, and when pressed too much comes
the vexed retort, " The grippa feeds itself upon its own
little fish."

(63)

" When you cook dogmeat eat it hot, for when it is
cold it smells badly." A Vai king announces that he
will carry war on the Golas, a neighboring tribe, but
he does not do so at once. He allows much time to pass,
and the Golas get prepared for the attack. In support

of abandoning the attack an adviser quotes among his reasons, " When you cook dogmeat eat it hot, for when it is cold it smells badly."

(64)

" A small string brings down a big bunch of grass." Mandingan grass is kept in the lofts of Vai houses. In taking down the grass by the blade, a single blade will almost invariably bring down a large bunch. A rich man injures several members of a family and escapes any punishment. By-and-by he does some little thing to another member of the family, and very heavy damages are insisted upon for this damage that is trivial in comparison with what he has done to other members of the same family and escaped without punishment. The man is now brought to pay for all the wrongs against this family through the occasion of this one little wrong, and astounded at the injustice of the claim he minimizes the wrong he has done; but somebody recalls to him that " A small string brings down a big bunch of grass."

(65)

" When you are troubled in mind and your slave runs away you put your hand in your pocket." A Vai man gets into serious trouble, and in his confusion of mind he goes for help to another man who is not his friend, and the man refuses to aid him. He relates the incident to a friend who reproves him for going to this man for help, and there we have an occasion for the saying: " When you are troubled in mind and your slave runs away you put your hand in your pocket," yet your slave is not in your pocket.

(66)

" You wash your mouth with cassava and it is good for the stomach." There is a custom among the Vais of eating raw cassava, and it is called washing the mouth. Among the Bussi people this is the chief way they clean their teeth. So that aside from being food for the stomach, cassava is really good for cleaning the teeth. A man is sick; the family has medicine to give him, but it must be prepared with fresh meat. The man has no appetite and does not wish to eat, but aside from the food he is told that medicine is prepared with it, yet he hesitates. But he is all right when he hears some one say, " You wash your mouth with cassava and it is good for the stomach."

(67)

" When an old lady goes to market the second time the first time she had good luck." A Vai man made a rice farm last year and he had bad luck, so this year he is making none. A friend who did not know of his bad luck but knew of the making of the rice farm is passing one day and inquires why a rice farm is not being made this year, and he is told, " When an old lady goes to market the second time the first time she had good luck."

(68)

" When one man has his stomach full it cannot satisfy every man." A rich man has a poor friend who works for his livelihood, and all the time the rich man either sends for him or he calls to have a stroll with him. But the poor man can ill afford to spend so much time in idleness, and so he begins to decline the invitations of his rich friend. The rich man, noticing the change, inquires, " What is the trouble? " Thereupon, the poor man answers, " You are rich, but I am a poor man. When one man has his stomach full it cannot satisfy every man. I must work for my living."

(69)

" Soon in the morning one man cannot go to two places." War breaks out between two tribes and one of the tribes has set a specific day for an attack upon a town. It turns out that this day is market-day. One of the men who is expected to accompany the attack remembers that it is market-day and informs those who are going to war that he intends to get his market and then join them for the campaign. The war people are not inclined to favor going to market before starting for the attack, and they object because it might delay the march and cause them defeat. The wisdom of the situation is found in the old words, " Soon in the morning one man cannot go to two places."

(70)

" The cow is larger than the horse, but the horse is more useful." The Vai singers are serenading the town. They visit a man who was born a slave but who is now rich, and he gives them ten dollars. Next they play and sing for a young man who gives twenty-five dollars. The singers are surprised to receive from this young man more than from the rich man, and comments are exchanged among the strangers. The young man is a freeborn Vai, a member of an old family of freemen, and takes great pride in his family history. The strangers will no longer be surprised when they hear him say, " The cow is larger than the horse, but the horse is more useful."

(71)

" If you run you crack your foot; they do not go together." The Vai man begins to plant his rice farm and he is hurrying so that he can cut palm-nuts; and he expeets to hurry with the palm-nuts so that he can go to trade. Some of his friends pass and wonder why this man is rushing so, and finally they inquire. As he relates his plans of getting rich in a short time somebody is sure to punctuate the story with this, " If you run you crack your foot; they do not go together."

(72)

" A man who has not seen the new moon before calls the stars the moon." A man is very poor and he has had to work hard for his living. But he has a stroke of sudden fortune, and is able to secure a little money, about fifty dollars, more than he ever had before in his life. He is so elated that he goes about boasting of his wealth and trying to put on airs. The rich people of the community who have been rich for generations feel a sense of disgust at the words and actions of this new lord of wealth, and they repeat among themselves the wisdom of the fathers, " A man who has never seen the new moon calls the stars the moon."

(73)

" A man can leave his house, but he cannot leave his way." A bad man has had so much trouble in one town that he has decided to move to another town far away where he is not known. When he arrives at the town he finds that his reputation for trouble has preceded him, and he hears with much surprise and regret what the people say; so he really decides to act well and to show that he has been maligned and misrepresented. He does very well for a time, but finally falls into his old habits, and the people begin to say, " A man can leave his house, but he cannot leave his way."

(74)

" The house looks pretty from the outside, but the inside is bad." The Vais like to dress, and some of the worst characters of the community appear in the finest and most costly dress. On ceremonial occasions some of these bad people appear so well that they excite the comment, " The house looks pretty from the outside, but the inside is bad."

(75)

" Old cloth has a new pocket." That is, a poor man suddenly gets a little money or is raised to position.

(76)

" The people are sorry for the man who plays the organ at night." That is, a man poor, with no wife nor other persons in his house, usually plays some kind of music at night when other people have gone to bed.

(77)

" A sassy woman puts chicken on the grave of her husband's friend." That is an expression that is used when some woman neglects her husband's grave.

(78)

" Noise of the horn is not news like the fire of the

gun." When a stranger, asked for news and knowing none, begins to say that the people are making a farm, this answer is often given to him, " Noise of the horn is not news like the fire of the gun."

(79)

" The piles always catch the thin, weak man." When people want to pass through certain tribes at war and they are warned not to pass that way, they reply, " The piles always catch the thin, weak man."

(80)

· " Man does not leave his well in rain time." New people come, and when one is about to leave old friends for the strangers the warning is, " Man does not leave his well in rain time,"— that is, when he has plenty of water.

(81)

" The rice bird finds a place to sit down first before he begins to eat rice." That is to say, before a person undertakes to do anything he should first get some power or make preparations.

(82)

" The little billy-goat never cries for horns." That is to say, a rich man's son never hurries like a poor boy to get money.

(83)

" You must hold the bamboo stick until you reach the country where you can get a reed." That is, sometimes you may have a bad boy, woman, or man, but you must hold him until you get a good one.

(84)

" Don't do me like the pestle that beats the flour." That is, a person claims something that belongs to a big man, but he never gets it. The pestle is white, but it has beaten no flour. So the big man says, " Don't do me like the pestle that beats the flour."

(85)

" The chicken cries for teeth, but he has not any." That is, when a man is promised to be made king he makes promises as to what he will do. In case he is disappointed and complains, the answer is made to him, " The chicken cries for teeth, but he has not any."

(86)

" Man walks through the bush by the word of a big monkey." That is, when a stranger asks in a town for some one to carry him to some king or place and they do not wish to do so or have no one to send they often say, " Man walks through the bush by the word of a big monkey."

(87)

" The elephant never gets tired of carrying his tusks." That is, no matter how poor people become they try to support their people, and if they complain the above words are echoed in their ears. If they complain when they are doing any other thing they ought to do they hear the words, " The elephant never gets tired of carrying his tusks."

(88)

" There is no sore as big as the head cut off." When

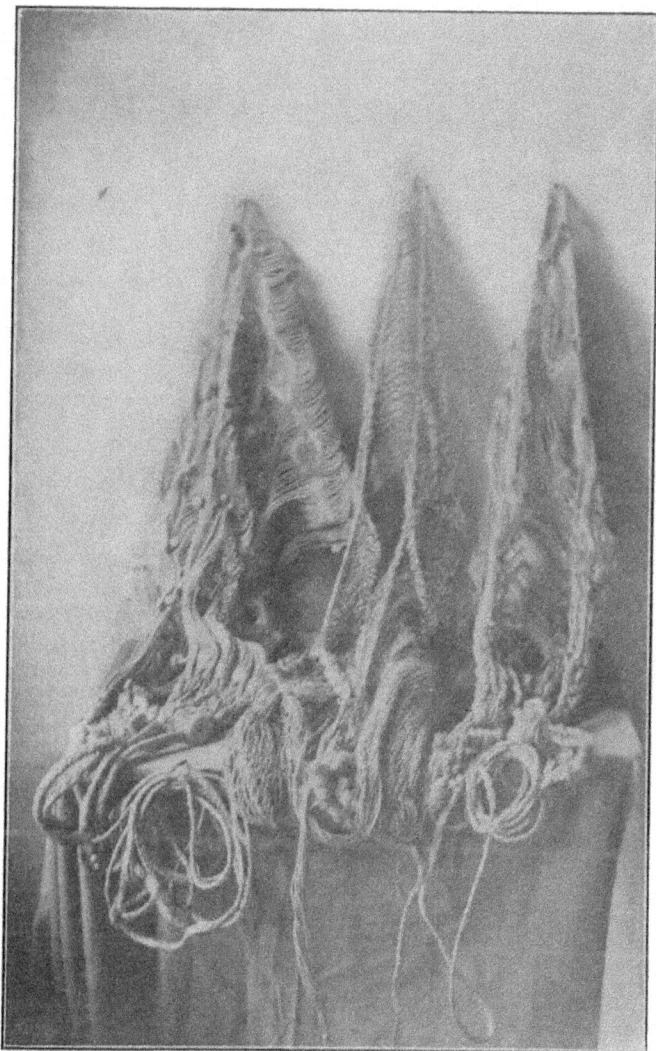

VAI GRASS HAMMOCKS

Facing Page

one man has done a great crime and some one complains of some smaller offense they are reminded that " There is no sore as big as the head cut off."

(89)

" The person who says catch a cat by the neck has been bitten before." When a person is about to stand somebody's bond and some one warns him not to do so and he wants to know why not, the answer is, " The person who says catch a cat by the neck has been bitten before."

(90)

" If the rain does not come the orange will still have water." When a person has become rich and refuses a favor and is told that certain trade will be withdrawn he replies, " If the rain does not come the orange will still have water."

(91)

" When you reach the head of the water the fish has finished." When a man owes many debts and all his property has been taken from him, and when some one says he will sue him again he is told, " When you reach the head of the water the fish has finished."

(92)

" If you put flour in two hands it will be dirty." When a person sends something to another person and gives it to a man to carry and he gives it to another, and he to another, and so on, when it reaches the person to whom it was sent some of it is sure to be lost. Therefore if any person proposes to transmit in this way he is told, " If you put flour in two hands it will be dirty."

(93)

" The fish likes water pass everybody." That is, when the king does some wrong and one of his own men or kinsmen admits it the opposers of the king say it is true because " Everybody likes water, but the fish pass all." The one man is likened unto a fish in water, and his testimony is more convincing, as the fish likes water beyond other people.

(94)

" The goat is not big in cowtown." When a man leaves his home and is unknown in a place, and especially when he is a big man at home and is not given the attention abroad that he feels he ought to have, he often says by way of consolation, " The goat is not big in cowtown."

(95)

" If the people say they will to-morrow kill the liar he cannot sleep." When a crime is committed and a day is set for finding out who did it and some persons flee before the time, the people use their parable, " If the people say they will kill to-morrow the liar he cannot sleep."

(96)

" Water does not clean a person's skin." When a man loses a case because he has not money to defend his rights and when people refer to him as being in the wrong as the reason why he lost the case, he answers, " Water does not clean a person's skin."

(97)

" The meat for every day is goat." When a person
who begs often considers too small what has been given
him the doner reminds him, " The meat for every day is
goat." That is, they cannot have beef and fine meat
every day any more than one can make large gifts often.

(98)

" The leopard cannot catch a person with a chicken
on his shoulder." That is to say, when a man has money
it is difficult to do anything to him. If some one complains that a rich man's son has committed a crime and
gone clear, he is reminded that, " The leopard cannot
catch a person with a chicken on his shoulder."

(99)

" One man who has eaten enough food is not sufficient
for other people in the town." One boy gets to brag-
ging about the rich men in his town and the poor boy
from a poor town answers, " One man who has eaten
enough food is not sufficient for other people of the
town."

(100)

" The little bird begins to cry before the other birds
come." That is, there is a bird with eyes far back in
his head and he begins to cry so as to shed tears at the
same time that the other birds do. This parable is used
when one man is chided for having been so long in build-
ing his house. He replies, " The little bird begins to

cry long before the other birds come," in order that he might have his house at the required time.

(101)

"People who kill an elephant do not forget the head." Two persons are friends, and one of them has something, and he gives it out to all but this friend. He comes and asks for his part, and the friend replies that he forgot him. The retort is, "People who kill an elephant do not forget the head." The head is valuable because it contains the ivories.

(102)

"The doctor-woman cannot take the baby for her pay." One person gives some things to be repaired to another who demands pay before he delivers them. He is told, "The doctor-woman cannot take the baby for her pay."

(103)

"You cannot lick your dry hand." You continue getting a man to do things for you and you fail to pay. Sometime you will ask him again to do something and he will remind you that "You cannot lick your dry hand."

(104)

"A snake has bad luck at the well." A man with a bad reputation is generally attended with trouble wherever he is known, whether he does anything or not; things that other people do are put upon him. When he is under some false accusation he often explains the injustice he bears by saying, "A snake has bad luck at the well."

(105)

"If you sit on the bottom of the sea, you cannot be a fish." One man comes to a strange place and talks assumingly concerning the affairs of the people. After he has resided there sometime, no matter how long, one day in discussion some one will tell him, "If you sit on the bottom of the sea, you cannot be a fish."

(106)

"It is not difficult to make a bag of a leopard hide." On important ceremonial days people dress their children. Good-looking children do not require so much dress. When the people are praising the good-looking girls some one who has spent a great deal of money in order to have an ugly girl appear well says, "It is not difficult to make a bag of a leopard hide."

(107)

"A minnow is not small to his deep." Often strange people will wonder how a small boy can be king or possess so much property, and the people answer, "A minnow is not small to his deep."

(108)

"A dried rat has blood." When a poor man gets rich or suddenly increases his fortune envy inspires many to say, "A dried rat has blood."

(109)

"You cannot tell a rock to strike where you desire."

A man has a bad son and everything he tells the son to do the son disobeys; then the people say, "You cannot tell a rock to strike where you desire."

(110)

"A man has a water-pot on his head, but he cannot drink." Often a man has slaves and they all go off to work. The master wants something done immediately; he calls some one to come and do it; they refuse. Then you can hear him muttering to himself, "A man has a water-pot on his head, but he cannot drink."

(111)

"When a man says, 'I savey sing he has his head.'" Sometimes when they have prisoners of war and the time arrives for execution some of the prisoners will claim that they will be very useful as slaves on the farm, and they will plead for their lives by telling the work they can do. Some of the captors, convinced by the pleas, repeat this parable in behalf of the pleading slaves, "When a man says, 'I savey sing he has his head.'"

(112)

"To eat raw is good for cassava." When a man brings stolen money or goods to the house of his friend they generally divide it. But if the money or goods be not stolen and the friend calls for a division, he is pretty apt to hear, "To eat raw is good for cassava."

(113)

"When you do not want to go in front or behind you have a messenger to carry you." When a man has a lazy wife who does not wish to do anything and desires the husband to hire a servant, when the time arrives to do some work she says she cannot do it. Sometime when she is saying that she cannot cook or cannot get water the husband reminds her of the fact that she has no servants by saying to her, " When you do not want to go in front or behind you have a messenger to carry you."

(114)

" To walk with nothing is better than to have a light load on the head or shoulder." Of a group of slaves two or three will combine to steal something. When the time for punishment arrives some will ask for light punishment because they only watched or knew about the stealing. It is then that the judge reminds them of their guilt and points out the superiority of the innocent man by the adage, " To walk with nothing is better than to have a light load on the head or shoulder."

GROUP OF NATIVE SINGERS

Facing Page 184

·VAI FOLKLORE STORIES

CHAPTER IX

VAI FOLKLORE STORIES

(1)

THE RIVAL SLEEPERS

TWO men met and engaged in a conversation, during the course of which one of them declared that he could outsleep the other. The second man denied that the speaker could outsleep him, and they made a bet after appointing judges that each could outsleep the other. The first man went home and built a big fire and laid down beside it to sleep.

While he was sleeping his foot caught afire and burned his leg to his knee, but he did not wake until some people, seeing him burning and fearing he would burn up, ran to him and awoke him, entreating the man to wake up, that he was on fire. He awoke and insisted that he was simply sleeping and that they should have allowed him to continue his slumber.

The first man had slept in spite of the fire that had burned his foot and leg to his knee, and on the next day it was the turn of the second man to sleep. He went home and laid down in the street beside his house and went to sleep. Before a great while it began to rain, and it rained so heavily that the streets were flooded and the man was washed into the sea asleep. No sooner had he reached the sea than a large fish swallowed him. This big fish swam up the river and was caught by the fisherman. As the fish was taken from the water and placed on the bank the people were astonished at the largeness of its abdomen. They hurriedly cut it open, and behold they found a man. They examined the man, found him alive, and woke him up. As he woke up he said, "I was simply taking a little nap; why did you wake me?" The judges were unable to settle the matter, so they submitted it to the people, who are still undecided as to which of them won the bet.

(2)

THE MAN AND THE GOAT

A man went into the forest and set a rope trap, and the trap caught a bush goat. The man was so eager to kill the goat that in his zeal he made a mistake, and with his knife he struck the rope and cut it instead of the goat, and the goat ran away. The man followed the goat for many hours; by and by both the goat and the man became tired; the man called to the goat to wait, and when the goat stopped the man said to it: "Twins cannot eat goat meat. My wife is a twin, my children are twins, and I am a twin. I do not wish to eat you. I was only joking." The goat said in reply, "If you, your wife, and your children are all twins and you did not wish to eat me, why have you followed me all these hours?"

(3)

THE THREE BROTHERS AND THE TOWN

Three brothers living in a town lost their father and their mother. They were so grieved over the death of their parents that they moved into the forest and built a camp. The oldest brother said, "I am going to make a rice farm." The next one said, " I will make a trap," and the third one said, " I want to die." The oldest brother made the rice farm. When the rice became full the bush animals began to visit the farm and eat the rice. The brother who made the farm told the brother who made the trap about the animals, and the trap was set on the farm. The trap caught one country pot. The next morning when the two older brothers went to the farm they saw the pot and the pot said to them, " If you come near or touch me you die." So they were afraid and went back to the house and told the little brother that since he wanted to die to go to the farm as death had come there. The little brother took his sword and went to the farm. The country pot told him what it had told the elder brothers, " If you come near or touch me, you will die." The youngest brother said, "All right; that is what I am looking for," and he at once broke the pot. As soon as the pot was broken a big town appeared. All the brothers claimed this town. The oldest brother said it belonged to him because he had made the farm, for if he had made no farm the animals would not have come and there would have been no town. The next one said: " Yes, you made the farm and the animals came, but you were not able to catch them. I made the trap that caught the town, and it therefore belongs to me." The small brother said: " No; the town belongs to me. You sent me to die and I went, and you two were afraid, so that by my going to die I met the luck of finding the town, and the town therefore is mine." They called the judge to settle the matter, and the judge said he could not decide and turned it over to the people who have not settled it yet.

(4)

MAN HUNTING

A man went hunting for game, and while he was out in the forest a heavy rain came up, and he went and sat down in an old camp. A deer came along, and the man attempted to shoot it, but the shot would not go, and the man took a little switch and began to flog it; then the shot went and killed the deer.

(5)

THE RACE FOR A WIFE

A man had a daughter who liked all the creatures of the forest. Each of them was trying to secure the daughter for his wife. They all went to the father for his consent. The father told them to wait, that he would place his daughter in the old field, and that the one who reached there first should have his daughter. They all agreed to enter the race. When they all assembled the Fox said, " We must catch the deer and tie him, or he will win the race, as he can run much faster than any of us." So they all combined and tied the Deer and started on the race.

After they had gotten on the way Mr. Spider came along and saw Mr. Deer all tied. Mr. Spider asked, " What are you doing tied? " The Deer told him how all the animals had combined to tie him in order to keep him from winning the race and securing the daughter of the old man. The Spider then said, " If I let you loose what will you pay me? " The Deer said that if he won the race he would give to him for his wife their first daughter. The Spider then untied him and jumped on the Deer's horn. The Deer ran and ran and finally passed all the other animals. When he got in the old field near the old man's house the Spider jumped down and ran to the girl. The Deer claimed that the girl belonged to him and the Spider claimed her, so they submitted the matter to the judge, who decided that the Spider won the race and therefore was entitled to the old man's daughter.

(6)

THE TWO BLIND MEN

Two brown men were blind, and they both took a walk. The one in front found a little horn and he blew it, and as soon as he blew it his eyes were opened and he could see. He said to the other blind man, "I found a little horn and blew it, and now I can see." He gave it to the blind man to blow, and he blew it and he could see also. But as soon as the second man obtained his sight he threw away the horn. The man who found it said, "Where is my horn?" The other replied, "I threw it away." "Give me my horn," replied the first man. The second man went and found the horn. "Here is your horn," said the second man as he handed it to the first man.

The first man was jealous because the second man could see, and he thought by blowing again he could be made to see much better than the other man. So he blew his horn again and became blind. As soon as he saw that he was blind, he handed the horn to the second man, saying, "I have fixed my eyes good past you; you fix yours now." The second man replied: "I do not wish to blow again; I am satisfied with my sight. Before, I could not see at all and I am thankful for the sight I have obtained; you keep the horn." The first man became enraged and demanded that the second man must blow or fight. "I cannot blow, and we must fight then," said the second man, whereupon he ran away and left the jealous man helpless and blind.

(7)

WHY THE ELEPHANT RUNS FROM THE GOAT

The Elephant told the Goat, "I am going to eat plenty of things past you." "No; I shall eat plenty past you," said the Goat. "Let us bet," replied the Elephant, "and to-morrow morning we will eat." The Goat agreed, and the next day they both went to a big rock. The Goat began to eat something, and the Elephant asked him what was he eating. The Goat replied, "I am eating the rock, and when I finish eating this rock I am going to eat you also." The Elephant ran, and from that day to this the Elephant runs from the Goat.

(8)

RIVAL BROTHERS

One woman had triplets. All three of them were good doctors. They started to go up the river. One of them said, "When I finish my patient I will not take a canoe to cross the river, but will cross so." The other two said, "If you do not take a canoe, we will not; whatever way you cross, we will cross also." They traveled until they came to a big river. The two brothers waited to see what and how the other brother would cross. The brother lighted his pipe and the smoke went straight across the river. And then the brother walked over on the smoke. One of the other brothers got a spool of thread, and making his thread bridge crossed over on it. The other got a bow and arrow and he shot one across into the bank; he shot another into this arrow and continued until the arrows made a bridge across the river, and then he walked over on it. So that all three passed over the river, but who knows the doctor work pass the other.

(9)

THE FLY, THE CRAB, AND THE MINNOW

The Fly, the Crab, and the Minnow took a walk one day. The Fly saw a palm-tree with ripe palm-nuts and said to the Minnow and the Crab, " Who is going to cut them? " The Crab said, " I will cut them." As she was climbing the tree the Crab had one of her little Crabs on her back, and it fell to the ground. The Fly saw the little Crab fall, and seeing that it was dead began to eat it. The Minnow laughed and his jaw broke. The Fly said, " I will go back to town and tell the people what we saw." When he got to town he called the people together and told them what had happened. As he came to town very quickly he was perspiring very freely. He went to wipe off the perspiration from his forehead and he cut himself on the head. So that whoever does a wrong thing must suffer in the end.

(10)

THE MAN AND THE CRABS

One old lady had a daughter. The old lady said, " No one can marry my daughter until he builds my house on top of the rock." So everybody tried to build

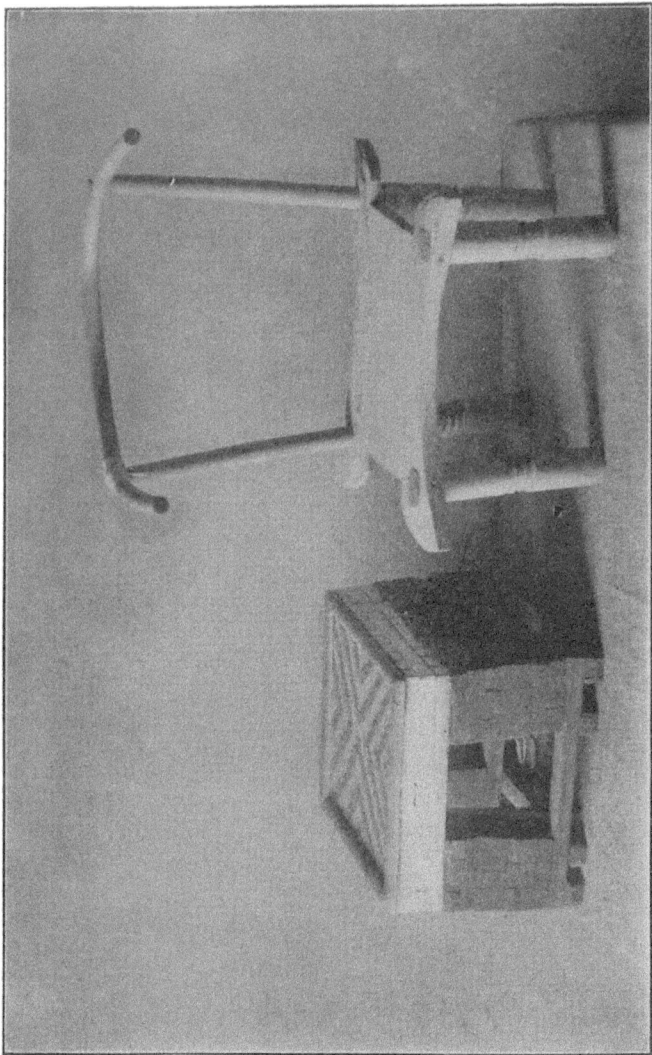

NATIVE CHAIRS

the house on the rock, but they all failed, as they could not stick the poles into the rock. So one man heard of the matter, and he said, " When I go there I will marry her." When he came he asked the old lady about what he had heard, and she said it was true. The man said, " I can build your house," and he brought his poles to the rock from the forest. He made a basket and the next morning he had plenty of crabs. He carried the crabs to the old lady and said, " You cook my crabs." She agreed and cooked them. When she gave them to him he tasted one and said they were not cooked done, he had brought his crabs for her to cook and she had not cooked them done. She said they were done. And the man said, " No; let us go to the judge." The lady said, " Judge, did you ever see crab cooked so that when you put it in your mouth you cannot hear it crack?" " No," said the Judge. Then the man said, " Judge, did you ever see a man before build a house on a rock?" The Judge said: " No. Why ask me these questions?" The man said: " The old lady said if I built her house on the rock, I could marry her daughter. I agree, but I cannot do it. So I take my crabs for the woman to cook and tell her that if they be done I will build her house. She agreed." So the Judge decided that the man had won the case and was entitled to marry the daughter.

(11)

THE RIVAL DOCTORS

There were three doctors,— two men and one woman. Each one claimed to be the best doctor. So the two men took one gun and went hunting in the forest. One of the men said to the other one, "I see an elephant behind that large rock." "How can you see an elephant behind so large a rock?" asked the other. "Never mind," the first man replied; "I see him." "Well," said the other, "you shoot him." So he shot through the rock, and killed the elephant. And then he said: "I have done my part now, and you must go and get him. You promised if I shot him you would go and get him." The other man said, "All right," and then he went to the elephant through the hole in the rock made by the bullet to the elephant, and brought the elephant back through the same hole. The woman doctor living in the town smelt the elephant, and without knowing where the other two doctors were secured the liver and cooked it. When the other two doctors reached town the woman doctor said to them, "Here is some breakfast I prepared for you." When they sat down to eat they found the liver of the elephant, and asked the woman, "Where did you get this liver?" She said, "You went hunting to-day and killed an elephant; that is his liver." Then all three of the doctors called the people and asked them to judge which of them excelled the other.

(12)

THE MAN AND HIS CHICKEN

One young man had one chicken and started to go where he heard there was one blind rascal man. "When I find him I will fix him." So he started out through an old field, and met the same blind man coming. The young man stood in the path and the blind man walked up against him and the young man's chicken began to holloa. Pretending that he was blind also the young man asked, " Who wants to take my chicken from me? " The blind man said, " That's all right; just give me the chicken." The young man, grumbling to himself, gave the chicken to the blind man. Then the young man went and found four rocks and returned. He took one in his hand and said, " Oh, Lord, if you be the true God, this rock must go and strike on the head of the one who took my chicken." Then he threw the rock and struck the blind man on the head. The blind man said nothing, but quietly moved to hide another place. He took another rock and said: " Oh, Lord, you are my father because I am blind. I can do nothing; but the person who took my chicken, I want this rock to strike him in the back." Then he threw and struck this blind man in the back. The blind man said nothing, but moved to another place. The young man took a third rock and said: " Oh, Lord, you make me and the person who took my chicken. You say you will look after the poor blind man. If this be true, then this rock must go and strike in the ribs the man who took my chicken." Then he struck the blind man in the ribs and knocked him down, and the chicken holloaed. The blind man said nothing, but finally got up and hid himself in another place. The young man took the last rock and said: " Oh, my Lord, I hear my chicken holloa this way, but I have not obtained it. You promised to come when called, and I have thrown three rocks, and if you are coming truly then this last rock must strike in the forehead the person who took my chicken." He then struck the blind man in the forehead. The blind man cried out: " Here is your chicken, come and get it. You are not blind. You have God in your pocket. You tell the rock to strike me in a certain place and it does it. Here, take your chicken."

(13)

THREE MEN WANT FIRST SMOKE

Three men took a walk. One had a pipe, one tobacco, and the third, matches. The man with tobacco said he wanted to smoke, but he had left his pipe and matches in town. The man with the pipe said he wanted to smoke, but had left his tobacco and matches at home. The third wanted to smoke, but he had matches with no pipe nor tobacco. The man with tobacco borrowed the pipe from one man and some matches from the other and prepared to smoke, when the man with the pipe claimed he ought to have the first smoke because he owned the pipe. The next man claimed the first smoke because he owned the tobacco, and the third man claimed he should smoke first because he had the matches and without them neither of them could smoke. They could not agree and they could not smoke and they began to fight. When they returned to the town all bloody they were taken to the judge to settle the matter. The judge heard the case and being unable to decide turned it over to the people. Which really of the three men was entitled to the first smoke?

(14)

TWO BOYS AND THE SNAKE

Two boys went to cut some wood. They had cut the wood and tied it up when a big snake came and bit one of the little boys, and he died at once. The other little boy cried and cried; finally he called the snake and told it that when he went back to town the people would think that it was he who had killed the other little boy. They would hold him responsible. He asked the snake to get some medicine and restore the boy, and then when his parents came he might bite them. The snake agreed and went and obtained the medicine and the little boy was again alive. The two boys got their wood and carried it to their respective homes. The snake followed this same little boy home, and bit him again, and he died shortly afterward. The people wept and wept; finally one man said they must stop and send for the other little boy and find out what his playmate had done in the bush to make the snake follow and bite him. They called the little boy, and he came and told what had happened in the bush, and how he had begged the snake to get some medicine to restore the boy so that he himself would not be held responsible. The people then called the snake to get medicine to revive the boy. They said: "You restored the boy in the bush because this little boy begged you to do so. Now all the people weep and beg you to restore him again. If you granted the request of this one little boy, you surely will not refuse the request of all the people." The little boy was restored.

(15)

THE RABBIT, BIG SNAKE, AND THE GROUND SQUIRREL

The Rabbit and the Big Snake made for themselves a big town in the ground. The Ground Squirrel came and said, "I want to stay with you all." The Snake replied, "All right; I agree." But the Rabbit said,

" No." The Snake asked the Rabbit, " Why do you not want the Squirrel to stay with us?" " Because," said the Rabbit, " this Ground Squirrel is a rascal; he does not sit down in one place; by and by he will bring trouble on us." " Never mind," replied the Snake; " the Ground Squirrel shall come and stay with us; I will mind you and I will mind your little brother. What is the matter? Are you jealous of your little brother?" The Rabbit remarked, " You have the power. All right; let him stay." So the Rabbit went and made a little hole by himself. Thus they lived for three months when the people came and made a farm near the town. Everything the people planted the Squirrel would get up soon in the morning and dig up; he took up the corn, the potatoes, the cassava, and the ground nuts. Every time the people got after the Squirrel he would run to the same place. So the people decided to follow him and catch him. All the people went after the Squirrel, and after digging a great deal in the ground they found him and killed him. They said: " This Squirrel is not alone. Plenty things live in this hole." So they dug on. The Rabbit whispered over to the Snake: " I told you so, but this trouble is your trouble and that of your son Squirrel, so I am going to my own little hiding-place." By and by the people found the Big Snake and killed him. But just before he died he said: " The Rabbit told me not to allow the Squirrel to stay with us as he was sure to make us trouble. If you fail to take good advice, you will pay dear for it in the end." The people, happy over having caught the stealing Squirrel and the Big Snake, did not dig farther, and the Rabbit was safe in his little home. Motto: " Bad company is sure to lead to trouble."

(16)

THE DEER AND THE SNAIL

The Deer said to the Snail, "I can run faster than you." "You cannot," replied the Snail. "I will bet you that I can," rejoined the Deer. "What will you bet?" asked the Snail. "Let us run," said the Deer, "and the one who loses, he and all his people shall be slaves to the other and his people." "I agree," replied the Snail. The Snail went and told all his people about the race, and stationed one at a certain distance apart along the way they were to run, and had one Snail stop in the town to which the race was to be made. The Snail knew he could not run and so he sought the help of all his people. But the Deer felt so confident of winning the race against the Snail that he did not tell any of his people. Having gotten all his people arranged, the Snail told the Deer that he was ready for the race. Off they went. About a mile away the Deer came to a river, and when he got there the Snail's brother cried out, "I am here too, and you must carry me across." "All right," said the Deer, "but I have not started to run yet." The Deer ran to the next river and a Snail cried out again, "I am here and you must carry me across." The Deer carried him across, and said, "I see I must run to beat you." So the Deer began to do his best in running. When he got to the next river the Snail cried out, "I have been here a long time, Mr. Deer. What have you been doing so long? You must carry me across too." The Deer carried him across, and started on his last run to the town. The Deer ran and he ran; at length all exhausted he reached the town, and as soon as he entered he saw the Snail.

The Deer holloaed and ran away without waiting for the judge to decide the race. And ever since that day when the Deer sees the Snail he is afraid and he runs.

(17)

THE TIDE AND THE MINNOW

The Tide came up and asked the Minnow, "What time does the Moon change?" The Minnow replied, "Oh, leave me; I am thirsty; I want a drink." The Tide said: "Minnow, what kind of foolishness is this you talk? You live in the water, yet you say you want to drink." The Minnow answered: "You came up and asked me what time the Moon changes; the Moon is up and you are up; you are related to the Moon, and if you call my word foolish, what do you think now of your question?"

(18)

THREE RIVAL BROTHERS

Three brothers took a walk. They stopped at a town and fell in love with the King's daughter, and each wanted to marry her. The King told them that he would give her to the one who brought him one slave. So they started out in search of the slave. They traveled many days into the country. One of the brothers had a glass into which he could look and find out each day everything that had happened in the town he had passed. One of the others had a hammock into which one might sit, and the hammock would carry him anywhere he wished to go. The third brother had some medicine with which he could raise the dead if they had not been dead more than three days. After they had walked two weeks in search of a slave one morning the brother with the glass looked into it and ascertained that the King's daughter was dead, and that she had died on the third day before. He told the other brothers the sad news. The brother with the medicine said that he could restore her to life if he could reach the town on that very day, before the third day had closed, but that they were more than two weeks' walk to the town. The other brother said: "That is all right. Come, get into my hammock." They all sat down and in a few moments they were in the town. They went to the King and asked what was the news. "Nothing," said the King, "except that my daughter you all like is dead, having died three days ago to-day." The brother with the medicine asked the King what he would give him, if he restored his daughter to life? The King promised him the daughter and all his wealth. The daughter was immediately raised from the dead with the medicine, and the brother who had the medicine claimed the daughter.

The brother who had the glass claimed her because, as he said, "But for my finding out that she was dead we would not have known that she was dead in time to restore her." "She belongs to me," said the brother with the hammock, "for although you knew she was dead we were two weeks' walk away, and but for my hammock we could never have reached here with your medicine before the third day closed." Unable to agree the brothers began to fight. The people came to part them and the whole matter was referred to the judge, who, unable to decide the case turned it over to the people. To which of the brothers did the daughter belong?

(19)

RIVAL STORY-TELLERS

Two men lived in a neighborhood and each of them heard that the other was a big story-teller. One day they met at a big dinner. When they had finished eating one of the men began talking; and among other things he said: "Things are small now, but when God created the world everything was big. I myself saw a big bird passing and the bird was so big that it took seven days before just its neck had passed." The other man braced up, saying: "I think you are right, because I saw one tree, and it was so large that God gave all the angels an ax and told them to go down and cut it, and they cut on it six months and did not cut it down." "Oh! it is not so," said the first man; "one angel is able to take this whole world, and what kind of a tree could it be that all the angels could cut six months on it and could not cut it down?" The second man answered: "Well, if God did not make this tree, where would your bird have to sit down? This is the very tree God made for your bird."

(20)

TWO POOR MEN

One poor man had some rice and he took it to one old lady to cook. She told him all right, but that she did not have any meat or fish with which to cook the rice. The man told her to cook the dry rice and he would eat it. The man went away. Another man came to the old lady with a bird that he had shot for her

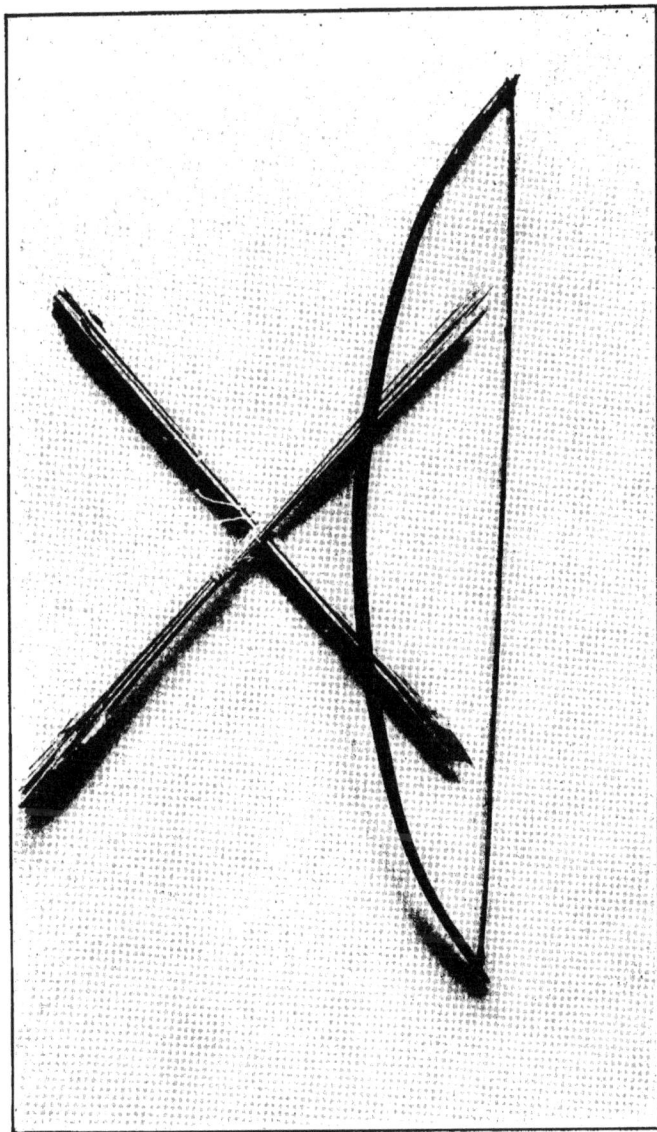

NATIVE BOW AND ARROWS

.

to cook; she said: "All right. But I have no rice with which to cook your bird." "Never mind," said the man, "just cook it so, and I will eat it." This man went out. The old lady cooked the dry rice and put it in a bowl for the first man, and the bird she cooked and put it in another bowl for the second man, and then she placed the two bowls together under a cover and went out. She met the first man, who asked about his rice. The old lady told him to go to the house and look under the cover and he would find his rice. The man went to the house, lifted up the cover, and saw his rice in one bowl and the bird in another. So he began to eat his rice and some of the bird. The second man met the old lady and asked about his bird, and she told him he would find it at the house under the cover. When the second man arrived at the house he found the first man eating his bird. "How you eat my bird?" said the second man to the first man. "No; the old lady gave it to me," said the first man. "She did not give it to you," said the second man, and they began to quarrel over the bird; then the old lady stepped in. The matter was referred to her, and she denied giving to the first man the bird. The first man contended that she did, and if not, why did she place the bird under the cover with his rice? Unable to agree, the case was referred to the judge upon a charge of theft. The first man contended that she gave him the bird, and the second man and the old lady that she did not. The judge decided that the first man was guilty, but popular sentiment was strongly in favor of this man. What is a proper decision in the case?

(21)

TWO MEN FRIGHTENED

An old man and his daughter were living in a town. The people began to take sick, and they all died one after another until the old man and his daughter were left alone. One afternoon the daughter took sick, and although the old man did his best for her by six o'clock she was dead. The old man was broken-hearted, and it was too late for him to go to the next town that night. So in his grief and despondency he left his daughter in the bed just as she died. The old man, bowed in sorrow, went to his room to rest until morning, but he could not sleep; for him there was no rest. As was his custom, the lover of the old man's daughter came to see her. She was absent from her usual place, and not a sound nor noise could be heard. As he approached the door he called the old man's daughter, but she answered not. Receiving no answer, the young man thought the old man and his daughter had gone out, perhaps to a neighboring town, but to be sure as he was leaving he thought to look into the daughter's room, and seeing her uncovered face he thought she was just asleep. Again and again he called her, but she did not speak. He entreated her to wake up, that he had something to tell her, but she did not wake. He asked her what he had done that she treated him so, but she slept on.

Finally the young man, talking to himself, became so loud that the old man heard him, and became frightened almost to death. He thought he heard the spirits of the dead of all the town gathered at his house. And talking to himself, he said: "Oh, Lord, since my daughter was born I have given her everything for which she asked. We alone in this old town have been left. All the other people die. But this afternoon she took sick and died."

As soon as the old man said the word " died," the young man himself became frightened because he had been talking to the dead, and he ran away. When the old man heard him running he attempted to make his own escape, thinking that his daughter's spirit wanted to catch him. They both ran to the next town, and told their experiences. The old man said, " My daughter died and her spirit wanted to catch me." Then the people said, " You sit down, and in the morning we will find out." The young man said: " I have been going to see the daughter of the old man in the next town. I went there to-night and began talking to her. When I heard the father say she was dead I became so frightened that I hastened away."

The people who heard the young man went and told the King, and the people who heard the old man did the same. The next morning the King called the old man and said to him: " What you reported last night is not true. One young man, a friend of your daughter, went there to see her as he has been doing before, and it was he that you heard talking. You take these people and go bury your daughter."

(22)

THE OLD LADY AND THE LITTLE BOY

The people of a town were having hard times and many of the people's crops had failed, so the King made a law that if anybody stole he was to pay a fine of fifty dollars; and that if any one is sleeping in the day time and some one wakes him up he must pay also a fine of fifty dollars.

The sun was hot, and one old lady took her cutlass and went to walk. She saw on the way one full plantain and she cut it. When she was cutting it and when it fell the owner heard the noise that she made. The man sent one little boy to see who cut the plantain. When the little boy got to where the plantain was cut he saw the old lady lying down asleep. The little boy shook the old lady and said: "Old Lady, Old Lady, wake up, wake up." The old lady awoke, and the little boy asked, "Who cut this plantain?" The old lady said, "Never mind the plantain; who woke me up?" The little boy replied, "I want to know who cut this plantain?" and the old lady insisted, "I want to know who woke me up?"

So the people came and took both the boy and the old lady to the court. The facts in the case were presented to the judge by the people, who asked, "Who was to pay the fifty dollars, the boy or the old lady?"

(23)

THE BLIND AND LEGLESS MEN

Two poor men lived in a town. One of them was blind and the other was without legs. The gifts that were made to the poor were hardly enough for two, so the man with no limbs wanted to get rid of the blind man so that he could get all. Whenever they went anywhere the blind man carried the other one, who pointed out the way. One day the man with no limbs said to the blind man, "Friend, we see a plenty of trouble. Come, let us go to the big river and drown ourselves."

The blind man said, "All right; I agree." The man with no legs got upon the shoulders of the blind man and they went to the river. When they reached the river the blind man asked, "Who is to die first?" The other man said, "I will die first." "All right, you go first," said the blind man. The man with no limbs instead of jumping into the river threw in a big rock. So the blind man asked, "Is it true that my friend actually has gone? All right, my time is finished, and I must go now. But before I die I must take my walking-stick and feel all around me." Then he took the stick and began to feel around, striking the bushes rather hard. When the stick approached the other man, the man supposed to be dead in the river cried out, "Oh, man, do not strike me with that stick." Then the blind man said: "What! You are not dead yet. You want me to die and yourself to live. All right; God helped me, and I did not die. Come; I will take you back to town."

(24)

THE SPIDER AND HIS MEDICINE

A Spider went to a Bird and said: "I want some medicine so that when I walk about I can do so quickly, so that when the people have big plays I can eat at all the towns the same day." "All right," said the Bird, giving the Spider the medicine with these directions: "When you want to go anywhere call my name first, —'Troo.'"

Very soon Christmas came and the people in all the towns were having big plays and killing fowls and bullocks for the dancers and the feast. The Spider woke early and wanted to go to Cape Mount, so he decided to try his medicine. He said: "Troo, I want to go to Cape Mount," and he was transported there almost immediately. When he arrived at Cape Mount the people were cooking the rice, fowls, and bullocks. The Spider said: "Well, I will not wait. I think the people in the next town have breakfast ready, so I will go on. Troo, I want to go to Mando." When he got to Mando the people were carrying the food to the King so that he might divide it. "What," said the Spider, "you have not divided the food yet. Why, I will go to the next town. Troo, Bomie." When the Spider got to Bomie the people had finished eating. "I am sorry," he said; "I will go back to Mando." The Spider had become very hungry. The Bird told him when he wanted to go extra fast to say, "Troo, Troo." So the Spider said, "Troo, Troo,— Mando." And at once he passed Mando and went on to Cape Mount, and when he arrived at Cape Mount the people had finished eating there. Finding that he had made a mistake by saying, "Troo, Troo," which had carried him too far, he simply said, "Troo, Mando." When he reached Mando the people had finished. Now why did not the Spider get something to eat with all the power of his great medicine of traveling with dispatch from place to place?

(25)

THE FOX AND THE GOAT

The Fox and the Goat went to a big meeting, and they put the two together in one house. So the Fox and the Goat got into a quarrel, and the Goat told the Fox that he intended to put him in a trouble out of which he

would never be able to get himself. The Fox said,
"All right; you put trouble on me, and I will return the
same to you." The Goat went for a walk, and he saw
a Leopard, and being frightened, he asked, "Auntie,
what are you doing here?" "My little one is sick,"
said the old Leopard. The Goat then said, "The Fox
has medicine that will make your little one well." The
Leopard said, "All right, you go and call him." So
the Goat went to the Fox and said, "They call you."
"Who calls me?" replied the Fox. "I do not know,"
said the Goat; "I think it is your friend. You take this
path and you will meet him." The Fox went down the
path, and at length came upon the Leopard. The Fox
became frightened and inquired: "Did you call me?"
"Yes, my son; your brother sick. The Goat came just
a while ago and told me you had medicine that would
make my little one well." "Yes," said the Fox, "I
have medicine that will cure your little one, but I must
have a little Goat horn to put it in. If you get me a
Goat horn I will let you have the medicine." "Which
way did the Goat go?" asked the Leopard. "I left
him up there," replied the Fox. "You wait here with
my little one, and I will bring you the horn," said the
Leopard. "All right," said the Fox, and away went
the Leopard. In a little while the Leopard killed the
Goat and returned with his horns to the Fox. You are
liable to fall in the trap you set for some one else.

(26)

THE OLD LADY AND THE BIRD

All the people had died in a large town but one Old
Lady. One day a big Bird came and inquired: "Who

lives in this town?" The Old Lady answered, "I am
here." "What do you do here?" said the Bird. The
Old Lady replied, "Plenty of people lived here; I was
rich; but they all have died now and I have no one to
help me, so I am helpless and poor." The Bird listened
and then asked, "If I help you, will you kill me?"
"No," replied the Old Lady. "Then just shut your
eyes," answered the Bird. The Old Lady shut her eyes,
and while they were shut all the people of the town who
had died waked up with their cattle, goats, fowls, and
riches. The grandchildren of the Old Lady were restored to her. When she opened her eyes she was hap-
pily astonished at the life and wealth of the once dead
town, and when the Bird said to her "This is all yours,"
her joy and gratitude knew no bounds.

The Bird says, "All right; I am going now, I leave
two eggs in this big tree. Watch and keep them for
me. If you do, you will never be poor again." The
boys of the town were playing, and one day they said
to the grandchildren of the Old Lady: "There are
two big, fine eggs in that tree," and they pointed toward
them. The little grandchildren went and told their
grandmother, and asked to have the eggs. The Old
Lady said: "No, you cannot have the eggs. The
Bird told me if I did not keep and watch those eggs I
would be poor and helpless again." So the boys began
to cry, and they cried and cried for three days, until
finally the Old Lady said: "Go and get one."

The boys went and got one of those large fine eggs,
cooked it, and ate it. In a few days they asked for
the other one. The Old Lady said: "How! You
want to kill me? You got one egg, why not leave the
other to the Bird?" The boys began to cry again

and continued until the Old Lady said, " Go and get it."

No sooner had the boys gotten the last egg, had it cooked, and eaten it, when the Big Bird returned. The Bird, finding no eggs in the nest, hastened to the Old Lady. " You try to kill some one who helps you?" asked the Bird. " All right; you shut your eyes." The Old Lady did not wish to shut her eyes. She faltered in the fear of the fate that waited her, but she had to close them. And with the closing of her eyes went the life, the people, and the wealth with which the Bird had blessed her. When she opened them she found herself again poor and helpless and looked out upon the silent streets of a town dead and lifeless.

Do not forget the means by which we rise.

(27)

THREE ROYAL LOVERS

One King had a very beautiful daughter. Three other Kings heard the news, and each of them decided to send his son to wed this charming maiden. The King in the East said to his son, " I want you to marry the pretty daughter of a neighboring King. Prepare yourself and go." So he gave his son many soldiers and attendants to accompany him, and the young man set out with his party for the royal maid.

The King in the South prepared his son for marriage, and sent him with his soldiers, fine dress, and attendants to wed the lovely daughter of this same neighboring King.

A King on the West prepared his son, decorated him with jewels, arrayed him in fine dress, and started him out with soldiers and attendants to marry this same royal and beautiful daughter.

They all arrived there on the same day. The King received them kindly. He called them all together and said: " You come from the East, you from the South, and you from the West. What is the object of your visits?" The young men gave the same answer,— they had all come to marry his daughter. So the King called his daughter and told her about the young men and the object of their presence. The girl said, " All right," and went back to her house.

For the young man from the East she had water prepared for his bath; she gave him clothes to make a change; and at night she supplied his bed with cover.

For the young man from the South she had prepared a big dinner and gave him and his attendants a royal feast.

To the young man from the West she gave nothing, but with him at sunset she went walking among the flowers and the trees.

A few days later these three young men met in the public square and their conversation drifted until they were talking of their favor with this royal maid. One of them said he thought he was going to win because the girl gave him water to bathe, clothes to change, and warm cover under which to sleep. The next one said he thought the girl liked him best as she had given him and all his attendants, a big, royal feast. But the other young man said, " No; I think she likes me best, for just at sun down in the woods by the lake we strolled together."

The young men were unable to agree, and they finally submitted the case to the judge, who said he was unable to decide the matter, and the royal maid is still unmarried.

(28)

TWO BAD YOUNG MEN

Two bad young men took a walk and went to see the King. One of the young men said to the King: "King, this young man says something that I do not believe. He says ' God has to give man everything,' so I named him ' God has to give man everything.' "

The other young man said: "Yes, I say that, King; and this young man says something that I do not believe. He says, ' Man has to give man everything,' so I named him ' Man has to give man everything.' "

"We want you to judge this matter," said one of them. The judge said: "All right. You must wait here ten days, and I will give you my decision. And when you come to hear the judgment I want each of you to bring me ten pounds." The young men agreed.

The King agreed with and was in favor of the young man who said, "Man has to give man everything," so every morning he put one pound in the rice and sent the bowl to this young man that he might get the ten pounds and verify what he had said at the end of ten days.

This young man when he received the rice would eat his portion and pass the bowl over to the young man who believed that God giveth everything. The one pound was at the bottom of the rice, and the young man who ate last got the pound every day, although the King was sending it to the other young man who received the rice and ate his portion and who believed that man giveth everything.

When the ten days were up the King called up the young men and told them he was ready to decide the matter. He asked each of them for ten pounds. The young man who believed in God handed him ten pounds, and the other young man who believed in man had nothing.

So the King ordered the young man who believed in man to be put in sticks. He said to the young man who believed in God: "What you say is correct. I have never believed it before, but I believe it now, because I sent that ten pounds for this other young man and you obtained it." To the other young man in sticks he said: "What you say is false, and you are confined that you may not preach your bad teaching."

God is the giver of Everything.

(29)

THE TWO FAITHFUL FRIENDS

Two friends, each named Kamo, had never seen each other; one lived in the East and one in the West. The young man who lived in the West went to the man who told fortunes by cutting sand and said, "I want to go over and see my friend whom I have never seen, and I want you to cut sand, so that I will know whether I will meet good or bad luck." The man cut the sand and told him that if he went to see his friend he would not find him home, but that he would meet him on the path, that when he reached the country of his friend he must not go out at night, no matter who called, and that if he did so he would surely die and never be able to return home.

This young man from the West was not satisfied with what the Fortune-Teller had told him, so he decided to go to another one, who cut sand for him and told him the same thing that the first Fortune-Teller had told him. So that when this young man heard the same words from two different Fortune-Tellers he believed it, and he said, " I will now go to see my friend, but I will mind what I have been told." He walked three days and met his friend, but he did not know him, and he asked him which way he was going. The young man from the East answered: " My name is Kamo. I am going to see my friend in the West, who is also named Kamo." The young man from the West replied, " I am he, and I am going to see you at your place." So Kamo from the East said: " You have walked three days and I have only walked one. Come; return to my place." Whereupon both Kamos went East, and when they reached there the same night a big snake swallowed Kamo of the East, so that Kamo cried and cried until Kamo of the West heard him and woke up. He wanted to go to the aid of his friend, but he remembered that the Fortune-Tellers had told him that he must not go out at night, so he sat down. However, he said, " I know I am going to meet trouble if I go out, yet I am going, because my friend is in distress." He went out and found that a big snake had swallowed his friend all but his head, so he took his knife and killed the snake by ripping his mouth open and in doing so some of the blood from the snake flew into the eyes of Kamo from the West and he at once became blind, while his friend was released from the grasp of the Snake.

Now Kamo from the East was free, but his friend who had freed him became blind in so doing, and he was sorry for his friend who had done so much for him. So Kamo from the East went to find a Fortune-Teller, a man to cut sand. The Fortune-Teller told him, " You have one son; go and cut his throat and take his blood for your friend to wash his face and then his sight will be restored." Kamo from the East went home, killed his son, and took his blood for his friend to wash his face that his blindness might be washed away. Kamo of the West washed his face in the blood of his friend's son, and immediately his sight was restored and his trouble was at an end.

Who was the greater friend, Kamo of the East or Kamo of the West?

(30)

THE ONE EYED MONARCH

One old King blind in one eye had ten rocks. He passed a law that everybody who passed his town must count those rocks, that if any one counted them correctly the people must catch him and kill him, and that those who failed to count them correctly he intended to kill. The first man to pass was called to count the rocks. He began and when he said, " One," the old King said: " Stop! I called you to count the rocks and you come to curse me. You say I only have one eye,— one. True, I have only one eye, but that is the trouble that God has given me." So he called his men, and had this man carried off and killed. Everybody who passed was treated in the same manner. By and by one young man said he had heard of the law of this old King and of the many people who had been killed under it ánd that he would go and break it down. One day this young man went to the King and the King brought out these rocks for him to count. The young man began. He picked up the first rock and said: "This,— no one can call its name in this country; if you do, they will kill you. So I cannot call its name," and putting it down, he continued to count two, three, four, five, six, seven, eight, nine, ten.

When the young man finished the people of the town rejoiced, and seizing the old King under his own law they killed him as he had killed many others before.

(31)

POOR MAN AND KING'S DAUGHTER

One poor young man lived in a town with his mother, who was a very old lady. The old lady was almost helpless and her son had to feed her. One day the King's daughter saw this young man, and she fell in love with him, and finally they married. After the marriage the young man ceased to feed his mother, and left this for his wife to do. So every day the young man's wife would feed and wait on the old lady.

One time when the old lady was being fed she caught the young lady's hand in her mouth and would not let her hand go. All the people of the town came and tried to get the old lady to let the young lady's hand go, but she would not. So they sent to call the young lady's husband. The young man came and he found out that it was necessary either to cut off the hand of his wife or to break the jaw of his mother. The young man was puzzled by the situation, and could not come to a decision in the matter. Some people advised him to cut off the wife's hand, and some advised him to break the jaw of his mother. But the young man could not make up his mind to do either. Finally the matter was carried to the judge for his decision. The judge asked the young people what under the circumstances would they do, and they said, "Break the old lady's jaw." He asked the old people and they said, "Cut off the young woman's hand." So the judge said that he was unable to decide the case. What would you do under such circumstances?

(32)

THE BLIND MORI MAN

A blind Mori man was living in a town, and he had a very beautiful wife. Every day the blind man's little boy would carry him to the mosque or church and leave him, and the little boy would return home. Somebody at the mosque would usually take the blind man home. When the blind man returned home after having been to the mosque he would eat his dinner, and the man who brought him home would eat also. One bad man found out that by taking this blind man home every day he could get his dinner for nothing. So this bad man would wait around every day until the people were ready to go home, and then he would go up to the blind man for the blind man to put his hand on his shoulder as he had seen him so often do when being taken home by some one at the service. By so doing the bad man got his meals free. One day this bad man saw the blind man's wife and he was charmed by her beauty and loveliness.

So he went to the King and told him that the blind man had a pretty wife, that although he was King he did not have a wife that could compare with the beautiful wife of this blind man, and that it was best for the

TWO KINDS OF VAI CANOES

King to take this woman from the blind man. The King wanted to see this beautiful woman, so he asked the bad man how he might arrange to see her. The bad man replied: " When the church is out and the people are leaving the mosque, you go up to the blind man and he will put his hand on your shoulder, then you go home with him." " If the blind man finds out that I am King, would not that be bad?" asked the King. " No," said the bad man; " all this time I have been carrying him home and he has never asked me nor found out who I am. The blind man will not know you are King."

That day the King went up to the mosque and went home with the blind man. When the blind man reached home they both entered, and the blind man's wife brought in the dinner. When the King saw the blind man's wife he fell in love with her. So he decided in his heart that he would do what the bad man had told him to do. When they had finished eating the blind man took the water in the glass and drank and he noticed that the water was bitter.

The blind man then turned to his wife and said: " This country is going to ruin, because some new thing has entered the heart of the King, and if he does it, then this country is finished." " How do you know? " asked the wife. " Because the water I just drank is bitter. Never before did water taste like this; so I know."

The King got up at once and went away. When he reached home he sent for this bad man who had told him of this blind man's wife. When the bad man had come the King said: " Why did you tell me to go and take the blind man's wife? Did you not know that he was a prophet? While I was there he told me everything that was in my heart. He told me that if I did what was in

Good

my heart the country would be ruined. So I cannot allow the country to be ruined, and this day you must die. If you are not killed to-day you will do something else that may ruin the country." So the bad man was immediately killed.

That same day the blind Mori man went to the King and wanted to know why the King had killed this man without a trial, since there was no war. So the King told him what the bad man had told him to do,— to get the Mori man's wife,— that the bad thing that he had had in his heart to do this bad man had told him to do, and that because of this action on the part of the bad man he had had him put to death in order that the country might be saved. The King also told him that the Mori man had spoken truly in his presence and that he was right. The Mori man was sorry that the bad man was killed, but it was too late.

When you plan to do some one else wrong you will not be free from injury and often will be the worst hurt in the end.

(33)

THE LITTLE BOY AND THE SNAKE

The people made a fire in a big old field and burned up everything. There were many animals that were caught and burned also. So every person went to get his part of meat. One Big Snake in trying to save himself went into a large hole in a bugabug hill. One Little Boy while looking for his meat came upon this Snake. The Snake told the Little Boy that he wanted the Little Boy to help him, and if he did, he would help the Little Boy in return. " There are plenty of people and many dogs here, and if I leave this hole," said the Snake, " they will kill me. So you must let me get into your bag and carry me into the bush." The Little Boy agreed, the Snake got into the bag, and the Boy carried him into the bush. After the Snake got into the bush he said, " Little Boy, I am hungry, and I think I will eat you just now." " What!" said the Little Boy, " you told me that if I would help you to get into the bush that you would help me by and by, and now you say you are going to eat me." " Yes; I know I told you that," said the Snake, " but when you leave you will change and grow so that I cannot know you to help you in the future, so I still think that I will eat you now." The Little Boy began to cry and continued talking to the Snake, when all at once came up Mr. Fox. The Fox asked, " What is the trouble?" The Boy told him, but the Fox said: " You tell a story, I do not believe you. How could this Big Snake get into your little bag? If you say so, Mr. Snake, come, get into the bag, and let me see." So the Snake came and got into the Little Boy's bag, and the Fox said to the Boy: " Did you say the bag was tied? All right, tie it and let me see." The Boy tied the bag and the Fox said, " I have finished my part of the work," when the Little Boy began to call the people from the old field. They came and killed the Snake.

Do not try to return evil for good, and always remember with gratitude those who lend you assistance or render you some deed of kindness.

(34)

THE TWO THIEVES

Two young men were living in a town. One of them said to the other one: " We are friends; let us go to stealing." The other young man said, "All right; but we must learn to be rascals first." The first young man said, "No, we must go and begin stealing now." "Come on, let us go then," said the other one. So the two started out to steal. As they came near a big town they saw a plenty of sheep. So the young man who first suggested the stealing caught one sheep. Some people saw them, gave the alarm, and a large crowd came out and caught them both. They were carried to the Judge for trial for stealing. The witnesses pointed out to the Judge the young man who had caught the sheep, who was the same young man who had first thought of stealing, and who had persuaded his friend to join him. So the Court began to question this young man about this stealing of the sheep. But the young man could say nothing. He was unable to make even an effort in his defense, and was at once confirmed and adjudged a thief in the minds of the people. So the Judge turned to the second young man to tell what he knew of this stealing of the sheep. The young man said: "This is my friend, Judge, and the matter is this way. I have been telling my friend as we were coming along that a sheep had lower teeth but no upper ones, and he did not believe me. So when we saw the sheep I told him to catch one, and he would see the truth of what I said. And that is why he caught the sheep." Those who steal will tell falsehoods, but the thief is sure to get caught.

(35)

THE FATHER AND THREE SONS

One old man has three sons. He went to another town and saw one girl that he wished for the wife of one of his sons, so when he returned home he told the youngest son about this girl and instructed him to go and see her.

So the young man went to see the girl. He arrived there at a time when times were very hard with the people for something to eat. They gave the young man a house in which to stay, water for his bath, and cover for his bed, but nothing to eat. The young man was very hungry. He saw some young cassava as he was coming along, and he became so hungry that he went back to steal some. When he came back with the cassava he forgot his house and went to the wrong place,— to the house of the girl's mother. He put his cassava in the fire, and while it was cooking he began to talk to himself. He said: "This girl's people must be poor people. They give me nothing to eat, and I must go and steal other people's cassava." So when he finished eating he wanted to lie down, and the old lady told him that he was in the wrong house, and when he found out that the old lady was the girl's mother and had heard what he said he ran back home. He told his father that the girl said she did not like him. He did not say anything about his trouble. His father said: "All right. I think she will like your next brother."

In a few days the father sent the next brother. When he reached the town he was given the same house in which his brother stayed. The people gave him the same things that his brother had had, and they treated him with consideration, but they gave him, also, nothing to eat. When the young man went to bathe he saw some ripe bananas on a banana tree, and he was so hungry that he thought he would just steal a few. The people had set a trap there for the bush cat, but the young man did not know it and in getting the bananas he got both of his hands caught. The people sent a little boy to the banana grove to get the bucket, and he saw the young man caught in the trap. The boy went back and told the people, and they came down and let him out of the trap. The young man ran home and told his father that the girl did not like him. " That is all right," said the father. " I think she will like your big brother."

So the father sent the big brother to see the girl. Like the other brothers, he was given the same house and treated with consideration, and as the hard times were still on they gave him nothing to eat. The moon was shining at night. He became so hungry that he went out too to see if he could not steal something. He saw some cassava in a large hole, but he did not know that the hole was so deep as it was almost full of water. He went in to get the cassava and could not get out. The people heard him swimming and wanted to know what he was doing there. He said he was just practicing swimming as he liked to swim so much. They threw down a rope and helped him out, and he ran to his father and said the girl told him she did not like him. The father said: " What! I will go myself and see what the trouble is."

When he arrived he was given the same house and treated like the sons. Food was still very scarce, and the people gave nothing to eat, and he also became very hungry. The next morning when he went out to bathe he saw one mortar where the people had been beating ground peas and had left some. The old man was so hungry that he put his head down to lick the mortar and his head was so fastened that he could not get it out.

The people called the girl to see what the old man had done. She was so ashamed of his act that she took off her ring and put it in the mortar, and when the old man's head was taken out she held up the ring and said that was what the old man was trying to get, as she had been telling him that he could not get her ring out of the mortar with his mouth.

When the old man got his head out he ran home and called all his sons together and told them that the girl did not dislike any one of them but that she said she disliked the family in general.

(36)

THE KING AND HIS BANGLE

A big King liked much to play a game called bŏh, but he did not understand how to play the game well. Every man who came to him he would ask him to play. One man beat him very badly, and the King gave him his bangle in pawn. The bangle was a large brass one, and was a fetich to the King, who regarded it as his life. The King told the man as he gave him the bangle that if he allowed any one to take this bangle or if he lost it that the King would be obliged to have him put to death. Near the town was a small lake which the King called his own and which was associated with his fetich. At night this bangle would come and go into the lake for the King, who would get it the next day.

The next day the King sent for this man who had his bangle and told him that he wanted to redeem it. The man replied that he had lost it. So the King, as he had told him he would do, had him put to death. So the

King did every man who beat him and took in pawn his bangle, and he thus killed many men.

One day one good young man came to see the King. The King's daughter fell in love with the young man, and each day she advised him for his safety. One day she was going to the farm and she called the young man and told him she was going to the farm for a while and that in her absence if the King called him to play bŏh that he must not play. "If you play," said the daughter, "Father will kill you." She told him how he had done many others, and why. The young man did not take the advice of the daughter and he played bŏh with the King, and as usual beat him and took in pawn the bangle of the King. As the King gave the pawn he told the young man that if he lost it he would lose his life. That night the young man lost the bangle. Early the next morning the King sent to the young man to redeem the bangle. The young man sent word that he had lost the bangle. The King then sent him word that he gave him three days to find the bangle. On the third day the daughter said to the young man, "Let us run away." He agreed, and they ran away. As they were running away they got very hungry and they happened to meet a girl carrying food for the people who were working on the farm. The daughter asked the girl to sell them the food, as they were very hungry. The girl said she was taking food for the farm hands, but if the daughter would agree for her to become also the wife of her husband that she would let her have the food. The daughter agreed and they ate the food.

The girl now joined them in the flight, and they continued their journey to escape. They walked until they became almost exhausted from thirst, when in the burning sun near an old field they met another girl carrying water to some people planting rice. The two wives offered the girl ten pounds for the water for their husband. The girl replied, " I cannot take the ten pounds, but I like this man, and if you consent for me to become also his wife, I will let you have the water." They consented and the girl gave them the water and joined them in their journey of escape.

They travelled and travelled until they finally came to a big river. They were unable to cross. They looked back and saw coming for them a large army of the King. Near by was a girl with a canoe. The three wives made up fifteen pounds and offered them to her to cross them. The girl said, " No; but if you consent for me to become one of your husband's wives, I will cross you." They agreed at once and were crossed. When the soldiers arrived at the river they were unable to cross, and the young man was free from the vengeance of the King.

By and by each of these four wives had a son. The father died. Each of the sons claimed his property. The son of the first wife claimed it all because his mother led his father in his escape. The son of the second wife claimed it because his mother gave his father food when he was almost dead from hunger. The son of the third wife claimed it because his mother gave water to his father when he was about to famish from thirst. The son of the fourth wife claimed it because his mother crossed his father over the river when the King's soldiers, pursuing him, had almost captured him when he was helpless on the banks of the river.

To which of the sons does the property belong?

(37)

THE MORI MAN AND THE SECRET

A Mori man was boarding with an old lady. One day the old lady ran out of food for the Mori man. So she told him she was out of food but that she had some dog meat; but the Mori man did not eat dog meat. She told him that he might eat dog meat just one day, and that if he would consent to do so she would not tell any one. So the Mori man agreed. But he said, " Just set my food aside for a while. Now you have some friends. You call your best friend,— the one to whom you tell everything,— before I eat." The old lady sent and called one woman who came. When the woman came the Mori man said: " Yes, I called you. But you call your best friend, as I have something to tell." So she called her best friend and the man came. The Mori man asked him to call his best friend and continued to do this until one hundred people had assembled. When they had all arrived the Mori man explained the situation to them. He said: " This old lady boards me all the time, but to-day she ran out of food for me, and wanted me to eat some dog meat upon the promise that she would not tell anybody. I consented, but I told her to send for her best friend to whom she tells everything before I eat; and she did so. When the friend came I asked her to call her best friend and he came, and so on until you see I have one hundred friends assembled. If I eat the dog meat this old lady will tell her best friend, and the best friend will tell her best friend, and so on until many people will know it. Therefore I cannot eat this dog meat." If you wish anything kept secret keep it to yourself.

(38)

· THE JEALOUS HUSBAND

One man was jealous of his wife who had two gentleman friends. The husband thought to kill the one of his wife's friends that he could catch at his house. So he told his wife one day that he was going away to a neighboring town, but instead he went to a house close by to watch. He had warned his wife about these friends, and she was afraid for them to call at her house, but she had had no opportunity to tell them what her husband had decided to do.

As it happened, on the day the husband said he was going away these two friends both sent word to the wife that they would stop by to see her, as they would be passing her home in the evening. So about six o'clock one of the friends made a friendly call at the house, and the wife, informing him of what her husband had decided to do in case he caught him there, told him not to call in the future. No sooner had she told him than her husband was seen coming home. Fearful of the friend's life, she tied him up in an old kinja she had in the house and stood him up in the corner.

When the husband came he asked, " What is that standing in the corner? " " It is a kinja," said the wife, " that one man left here this afternoon and said he was coming back for it, but as yet he has not returned. I do not know what is the trouble."

Very shortly afterward the other friend stopped by, and, knowing the jealousy and intention of her husband, the wife met him at the door and said: " What has been the matter that you have just come back.

Here, take your kinja." The man, seeing the husband and noticing the temper of the wife, could see that something very serious was the matter, and without any question he took up the kinja and went away.

After they had got some distance from the house the man in the kinja said, " Oh! man, put me down." The other man was startled and put him down. When the man got out of the kinja he said to the other man: "You came near being killed. If it had not been for me in the kinja, you would have been killed this night," and then he told the other man what the wife had told him the husband had said. The other man replied, " Yes, and if it had not been for my carrying you away, you would have been killed yourself." Each man had helped the other and each had had a narrow escape.

Be careful how you call on other men's wives.

(39)

THE MAN, THE DEER, THE 'POSSUM, AND THE SNAKE

A man cut his farm and planted plenty of cassava, and the Deer always came to the farm to eat this cassava. He made a trap and set it for the Deer. The Deer was caught one day. The man went and found the Deer in the trap. He started to kill the Deer, and the Deer told him he must not kill him. " If you let me go," said the Deer, " I will make you rich." The man took the Deer out of the trap. The Deer told the man to lay on his back. The man did so, and the Deer carried him far away into the big bush near a large town and left him there.

The man had a piece of cassava in his hand when he was carried into the bush, and while he was eating it that night a 'Possum came to him and told the man if he would give him a piece of the cassava he would make the man rich. The man gave him a piece and the 'Possum went to the town and went into the King's house. The King had plenty of cola there in a jar. The 'Possum broke the jar and took the cassava and strewed it all the way to the man in the big bush. The people woke up and saw this cola scattered along, and they followed the line of the cola to the man. The people caught this man, and carried him to the King, and the King put him in sticks.

While the man was in sticks he made another trap and caught two rats. A Snake came to the man and told him, " If you give me these two rats, I will make you rich." The man gave the Snake the rats and the Snake went and bit the King's son. The King was worried and called all the people and told them if anybody gave him medicine to cure his son he would give that person one half of his town. The man in the sticks told the Snake, and the Snake gave him medicine to cure the King's son. The man went and cured the King's son, and the King divided his town in half and gave one half to the man who cured his son. The man was now rich. The Deer came and said he had made the man rich. The 'Possum came, and he claimed that he had made the man rich, and finally the Snake came and contended that he had made the man rich.

Which of the three, the Deer, the 'Possum, or the Snake, did make the man rich?

(40)

THE LION, THE FOX, AND THE MONKEY

One day three men caught a Lion and dug a deep hole

and put the Lion in it. They left the Lion, and the Fox came by. The Lion told the Fox, "If you take me out of this hole, I will make you rich." The Fox replied that his family had sworn not to go into any hole, and then he went on. The Monkey came along, and the Lion told him that if he would take him out of the hole, he would make him rich. The Monkey said, "All right. I will try." The Monkey went up and caught a large limb and bent it down into the hole, and the Lion came out on it. When the Lion was up out of the hole the Monkey said to him, "Now make me rich." The Lion replied: "I am hungry. I have been in the hole three days. If you will give me something to eat, then I will make you rich." The Monkey answered: "What have I got here to give you? I have nothing you can eat."

"Yes, you have," said the Lion. "You have a long tail, you can give me a piece of that." "How can I give you a piece of my tail without killing myself?" asked the Monkey. The Lion became angry, and catching the Monkey, killed him.

While the Lion was killing the Monkey, the Monkey told him that he would not be able to catch any monkey besides himself, and all the other monkeys went up the tree. And since that day no lion has been able to catch any monkey.

(41)

TWO GREAT SWIMMERS

One man had three cows and three boys, and he said, "If anybody can beat me swimming in this country, I will give him all." And everybody who could swim tried to beat this man swimming, but they could not. And then this man was known as the best swimmer in his country. The news went far and wide.

So one day another man in another country heard about this man's swimming, and as he could swim too he thought he would try to outswim him. So the two men met and agreed to swim on a certain day; three cows and three boys were to go to the winner. The second man went back to his country and told his people about the swimming match. His people asked him if he thought he could beat this first man swimming,— the one whose reputation for swimming had travelled so far and wide. The second man replied that he thought he could. "But how can you do that?" asked his people. "Never mind; I will do it," said the man. Then he told his people that he wanted ten kinjas of rice, ten kinjas of cassava, three bunches of plantain, and four pots, and when he got them he set out with his people for the country of the first man.

When he arrived he said to the great swimmer, "I am ready now to swim against you." The first great swimmer said, "All right; we will swim to-morrow." The two men went to the waterside where all the people of both countries had gathered. The second man carried all his kinjas of rice, his kinjas of cassava, his bunches of plantain, and all his pots to the waterside. He then tied all these in one bunch and put them on his back, when the other man said, "What are you going to do with all those things on your back in the water?" "What do you think?" said the second man. "This is the way we swim in our country. We carry our food and when we get hungry we eat." " We do not know how to swim like that in this country," said the first man, " and if that is the way you swim, you can beat me, so the cows and boys are yours."

Intellect is greater than muscle.

(42)

THE TWO FIGHTERS

One man liked to fight, and he whipped everybody he met. He took three cows and went about his country, offering these three cows to anybody who could whip him.

One lazy man heard about this man's fighting, and came to him and told him that he could whip him. " Before we fight," said the lazy man, " we must bet. I will bring my three cows and the one who whips will take the six." The champion fighter said, " All right; we will fight to-morrow." The lazy man before he started to the fight told his boy that if the fighter struck him four good licks he intended to run. " All right," said the boy; " let us go." The two men met to fight. And they began to fight; the champion fighter struck the lazy man four strong blows when the lazy man cried out to his boy, " The time has come." The boy said, " Wait until he strikes you one more time." Then the great fighter said to himself, " This man wants to wait until I strike him again before he does what he intends to do, he surely means to kill me," and he at once stopped fighting and ran. And the lazy man won the six cows and the fight.

The fight is not always to the strong but to him who holds out to the end.

(43)

THE TWO BROTHERS

There were once two brothers. The large one said to the little one, " Let us go into the bush and stay, because we have no one to help us and we must go to find some one." The brothers then went into the bush. The large one knew how to make a trap, and he caught a plenty of meat to eat. The little one knew how to make cloth, and he made cloth all the time. When the large one told him, " Let us go see about our trap," he said, " No; I am making my cloth."

When the large brother would go to his trap he would always find one woman that had come from the bush standing there. The woman would always bring rice and set it down by the trap and the large brother would eat it when he came. One day he said to his little brother, " Every time I go to the trap I meet one woman there who always brings rice to me." The little one asked, " Has the woman cloth?" " No," said the larger brother. " When you go next time you must tell me," said the little brother. The next morning the two went to the trap. They saw this same woman standing there. The large brother asked the woman to come to them. " I cannot," said the woman, " as I have no cloth." " I can give you some cloth," replied the little brother. The woman came and the little brother gave her some cloth, and she tied it upon her waist, and the three together went where the brothers stayed. " But for me we could not have obtained this woman," said the little brother.

" No," said the larger one. " I saw her first, and she belongs to me. Because if I had not made my trap, we could not have secured this woman." " Were you not going to your trap all the time? And you saw her, and could not get her," said the little brother. So the two brothers had a big fuss about the woman, and finally they went and told the King.

The large brother said, "This woman belongs to me." "How did you get her?" asked the King. "I made a trap and put it in the bush, and every morning I found this woman standing near by," said the larger brother. "Yes, you made your trap and found this woman, but when you called her she would not come, and had I not given her my cloth she would not have come," answered the little brother. The King said to the little brother, "You let the large brother have this woman, and let him make another trap, and the next woman he finds belongs to you." "All right," said the little brother, and they left.

When the two brothers arrived home they met another woman sitting down, and the little brother gave her one of his cloths, and the large brother consented that the little brother might have this woman, as the King said he should have the next one that was found. Now both had wives and everything went well with them.

Man can afford to be generous with his brother.

(44)

TWO UNFORTUNATE MEN

There were two men: one was blind and the other one had no limbs and could not walk. The man who could not walk knew how to shoot, so he told the blind man if he would carry him into the bush that he would shoot some meat. The blind man put the lame man on

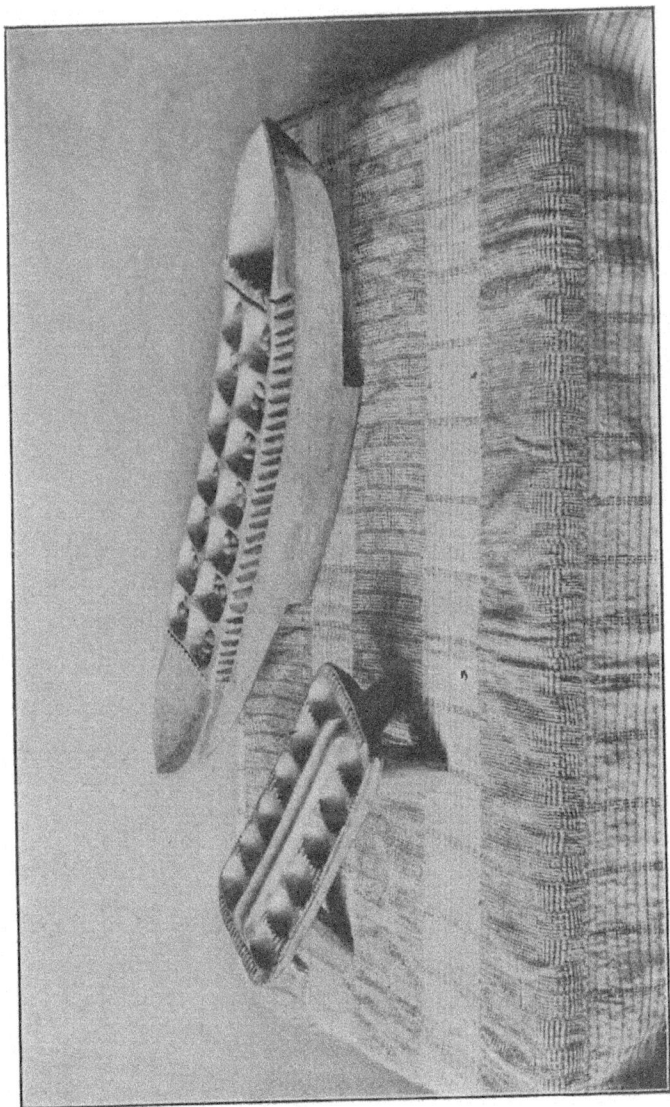

VAI CLOTH AND GAMING BOARDS

Facing Page 236

his back and carried him into the forests. The lame man saw one big deer and killed it. The blind man asked, " Did you kill him? " " Yes," said the lame man. Then the blind man carried the lame man to the deer. He put the deer in a kinja and carried both the deer and the lame man to the house.

When they reached home the lame man took all the meat for himself. The blind man asked that a small piece of the deer meat be cooked for him, but the lame man, knowing that the other man was blind and could not see the meat in the house, said that he had sold all the meat, when in fact he had it all there in the room. He took a piece of the deer skin, cooked it for the blind man, and gave it to him. " Ah," said the blind man, " all this large deer you killed and I must eat so-so skin." Thinking only the skin was left, the blind man tried to eat it, and as he was eating it the skin jumped out of his hand and mouth and struck him in the eyes, and his eyes were opened and he could see.

He looked around and saw all the deer meat. Then he said to the lame man, " Did you not tell me that you sold all the deer meat when here it is all here? " Then he went out and cut a switch and came back and began to whip the lame man. All at once the lame man regained his legs and was able to walk.

The lame man said he was the cause of the blind man's being restored to his sight, and the blind man said that he was the cause of the lame man's being able to walk. So they carried the matter to the King, who said that they should let the matter drop, as each had saved the other.

You cannot hide dishonesty.

(45)

THE LION, THE LEOPARD, AND THE DOG

The Lion, the Leopard, and the Dog were living together. They heard the news that the Goat had built a big town. The Lion said to the Leopard: "We had better carry war on that town, as we have nothing to eat." So the two joined and carried war on goat-town. They fought a whole day and were unable to take the town and were driven back. They went back and told the Dog of their misfortune and that he must join them in another attempt to take goat-town. The next morning the three went and after fighting all day they took the town.

When they went into the town they found only one Goat and one Cat. The Lion caught the Goat and the Cat and said they were going to carry them. The Cat did not wish to be tied, and asked to be left untied so that he could dance. The Lion said, "All right." Then the Goat said, "You should leave me untied as I am a doctor." So they left both untied. "Let me see you dance now," said the Lion. The Cat began to dance and he danced well. Then he said, "I can jump." "Jump then," said the Lion. The Cat jumped over the barricade and ran into the bush.

The Lion turned to the Goat and said, "You say you are a doctor. Well, the Cat has run away. I want you to try your medicine, so that we can catch him." Then the Lion, the Leopard, and the Dog all closed up around the Goat to prevent his getting away like the Cat. The Goat told the Lion to bring him one large pot. The pot was brought. The Goat put his hand in his bag, and he took out one bottle filled with honey. He placed the honey in the pot. "You must put a cloth over me and the pot," said the Goat. The Lion did not know that the Goat had honey; he thought it was water in the pot. The Goat took a spoon and gave the Lion some of the honey in the pot, saying, "This is some of the water my medicine gave me."

When the Lion tasted the honey he said, "Oh, you are a doctor for true." The Lion said, "I know you are a doctor now, so make me some medicine to wear around my neck." The Goat told the Lion that the medicine they wear around the neck is put up in leopard skin, and that he must kill the Leopard so he could get some of the skin. "All right," said the Lion. The Lion started after the Leopard, and the Leopard ran, and the Lion after him, and the Dog followed. So the Goat made his escape back the other way.

So the Lion dislikes the Leopard, the Leopard dislikes the Goat, and the Goat dislikes the Dog.

(46)

THREE STORY-TELLERS

Three story-tellers met one day and began to tell stories. Each of them thought that he could excel the others. The first man said, "I will tell you the story of what I saw.

"One day I went into the field and saw two birds fighting. One bird swallowed the other, and then in turn was swallowed by the other bird, so that the two birds swallowed each other."

The next one said, "One day I was going out to the

field and I saw a man on the road who had cut off his own head and had it in his mouth eating it."

The third man said, " I was going to a big town and I saw a woman coming from the town with a house, a farm, and all her things on her head. I asked the woman where she was going, and she told me she had heard news that she had never heard before. I asked her what it was. The woman said she had heard the news that one man cut off his head and had it in his mouth eating it, so I was afraid and left the town. The woman passed and I went on."

Who told the biggest story?

(47)

THE LEOPARD AND THE GOAT

One day the Goat was walking about in the field, and he met the Leopard. The Leopard told the Goat, " You must tell me three truths so I can save you." The Goat replied: " The first truth is that your stomach is full. Were it not for that you would kill me just now." " That is one of the truths," said the Leopard. " The next one is if I had known that you were here I would not have come this way," said the Goat. " That is two," said the Leopard. " If I go and tell any of my brothers that the Leopard and I met to-day, they would not believe me." " That is true," said the Leopard. " Well," continued the Leopard, " since it is true that if you tell any one that you and I met to-day and it will not be believed, I think I had better kill you." " All right," replied the Goat; " but let me go and call the Dog, so that he can be our witness." " Very well; go call the Dog," added the Leopard. The Goat went and told the

Dog that the Leopard had said, " We must go and make medicine for him." " No, I am not going anywhere," replied the Dog; "the Leopard does not know me." Then the Goat left the Dog and ran into the town, and ever since then he has been stopping in town. The Leopard had the Cat with him and he told the Cat to go and look for the Goat, and the Cat came to town and has not returned. So the Leopard likes neither the Goat nor the Cat.

(48)

TWO OLD WOMEN

There were two old women living together. They were very greedy and loved to eat, but they did not like to work. One of them said to the other one, " Let me go into the bush and find something to eat for us." " Go on," said the other woman, and she went. The woman went into the bush and she saw hanging in the tree many bowls of rice. She did not know how to get this rice, it was so high up in the tree. So she went back and told the other woman about her having seen the rice in the tree. The woman replied, " You may go on and get your rice, but I am going to stay here and wait on God." " Well," answered the other woman, " you cannot tell me where I can get medicine to get some of the rice." " I hear," continued the woman waiting on God, " that the Fox has medicine." The woman then went to see the Fox. The Fox told the woman, " To-morrow morning we two will go to the tree." The next morning the Fox and the woman went to the tree. When they reached the tree the Fox got his medicine, and he brought down one of the small bowls of rice. On each bowl of rice was a bunch of switches, small ones on the small bowl of rice and large ones on the large bowl of rice. And before eating the rice the switches had to whip you. The Fox said to the woman, "You asked me for medicine. I have given you the medicine and brought down the rice, can you stand the whipping that is necessary?" "I did not know you had to stand a whipping first," answered the woman. "I do not think that I can stand the required whipping."

So the Fox left and went into the town. When he arrived there he found the woman waiting on God sitting down eating rice. "Where did you get this rice?" asked the Fox. "God gave it to me," she said. Then the other woman came up, and seeing that this woman had obtained rice while she was sitting down in town, she said, "I think I had better wait on God too," and she sat down. "I see now," she continued, "that you cannot get anything unless God gives it to you."

(49)

TWO ORPHAN BROTHERS

Once a man had two sons and he died. Before he died he called his sons to him and to the large one he said, "If your brother tells you to do anything you must do it, no matter what it is," and then the old man passed away.

The little brother told the large one that they must go in the bush and live there as they had no one in the town. "All right; let us go," said the large brother, and they went. When they got in the bush some distance they saw the lion lying down sleeping. The little brother said to the other, "Let us kill this lion." "But what have we to kill him with?" asked the large brother. "We have no gun nor anything else." "I have a bow and arrow," replied the little brother. "But," said the other, "can bow and arrow kill a lion?" "That is all right," continued the little brother. "When father was dying did he not tell you to do everything I told you?" "Well, shoot the lion with your arrow," said the large brother. The little brother shot the lion with his arrow; then the lion jumped up and ran after the two brothers. The brothers climbed up into a large tree, and the lion left them there.

After the lion left they did not know how to come down, and while they were there the Eagle came by. The large brother asked the Eagle to carry them out of the tree. The Eagle said, "You two get on my back," and they did so. The Eagle flew away with them and carried them into a field where there were plenty of rocks. The little brother said he was going to shoot the Eagle so they could fall down and die. "You must not do that," said the large one; "if you do, we will fall down on those rocks and we will die." "Did not my father tell you to do whatever I said?" asked the little brother. The large brother said, "Well, shoot him." The little brother shot the Eagle. They fell down on the rocks and both of them died.

A Snail came along and found them dead. The Snail went into the bush, got some medicine for the large brother, and he got up. The Snail then asked if he must make some medicine for the other brother. "No," answered the large brother; "because my brother is a bad fellow. He has gotten me into a plenty of trouble. Come, let us go." "You are as bad as your brother," replied the Snail, "because you say I must not cure him." "Well, cure him and you will see," concluded the large brother. The Snail gave the little brother some medicine, and he at once arose, and as soon as he got up he said he was going to kill the Snail. "You see; did I not tell you?" remarked the large brother. The little brother took the Snail in his bag and said to his brother, "Let us go on."

They went into a large town. After they arrived at the town they heard that the King was dead. The little brother said, "You must tell these people that we killed the King." "We have been dead once, and you want us to die again?" said the large brother. "Did not father say that anything I say you must do it?" asked the little brother. "Well," added the large brother, "you go tell the people that you killed the King." The little brother went and told the people, "I and my brother killed the King." The people caught the two brothers and put them in sticks. The little brother said to the people, "You must carry us into the house where the King is." The people did so. Then the little brother continued: "We killed the King. But what will you give us if we cure him?" The people answered, "If you cure the King, we will give you half of this town."

The little brother took the Snail that cured them from his bag and told the Snail that he must use his medicine to cure the King. The Snail cured the King. He then called all the people and told them, "I have cured the King." The people divided the town in half and gave the little brother half. Then the little brother told the large one that he must stay there while he had to walk about, as he had given the larger brother plenty of trouble. The little brother left the town and killed the Snail.

All is well that ends well.

(50)

CONTROVERSY BETWEEN TWO MEN ON THE RELATIVE VALUE OF EDUCATION AND MONEY

By Momoru Duclay

Affirmative. Money is fine. It pass book sense.

Negative. Book sense is fine. It pass money.

Affirmative. Money is fine and I live to go and find my money.

Negative. Book sense is fine and pass the money; that is why I go and find book sense. Because book sense is property for the prophets. Money be property for Pharaoh in this world.

Affirmative. Money is fine. Money be property for the prophets in this world. Prophet Abraham built one great house for God with gold and silver and painted it red, and placed on the inside a sweet smelling substance. Now Abraham did not take the Bible and build the house?

Both men now go to find a judge by the name of N'fah Boikai Selekee.

Negative. Judge N'fah Boikai, book sense is fine, pass money. Because if you don't know the God book what thing can you know in this world, for when you die what thing you know again? If your mind know book what thing you lost that you cannot see?

Affirmative. Judge N'fah Boikai Selekee, money is fine pass book sense, because money can carry you for Allekamba; book sense not fit to carry you to Allekamba.

Judge Selekee. You both tell truth. You all go for one Judge Ahmala, he will cut this palaver for you all two, because this judge has plenty of sense.

They go for Judge Ahmala.

Negative. Tells the judge! We come to you, book sense is fine pass money, because if a person die you can call book man to come and preach for die man. You can't say call money man to preach for this die man.

Affirmative. Money is fine pass book sense because if a person die he can say where is the cloth with which to bury the die man? You can't say where is the book sense for to put on the dead man, you say bring the cloth.

Ahmala. You all two tell the truth, but you go to one Judge N'fah Asumana, because he has got plenty sense too much, he be professor for book. All two go again. They are going for this judge.

Negative. Book sense is fine pass money, because if you know book, book sense will help you in this world; will give you sense to pray to God in this world. Because money can make you forget God.

Affirmative. Money is fine, it pass book sense, because if you no got cloth, you can't go to church; if you no got money, you can't eat nothing; if you no eat nothing, how you fit to walk and go to church; and if you no got good gown, how can you go to church?

N'fah Asumana. You all two done tell the truth, but go for one man Alihu, because this man be man for book pass all we.

All two go for Alihu.

Negative. N'fah Alihu, book sense is fine pass money, because on Sunday you can say go call the man who know the book to preach. You can't say go call

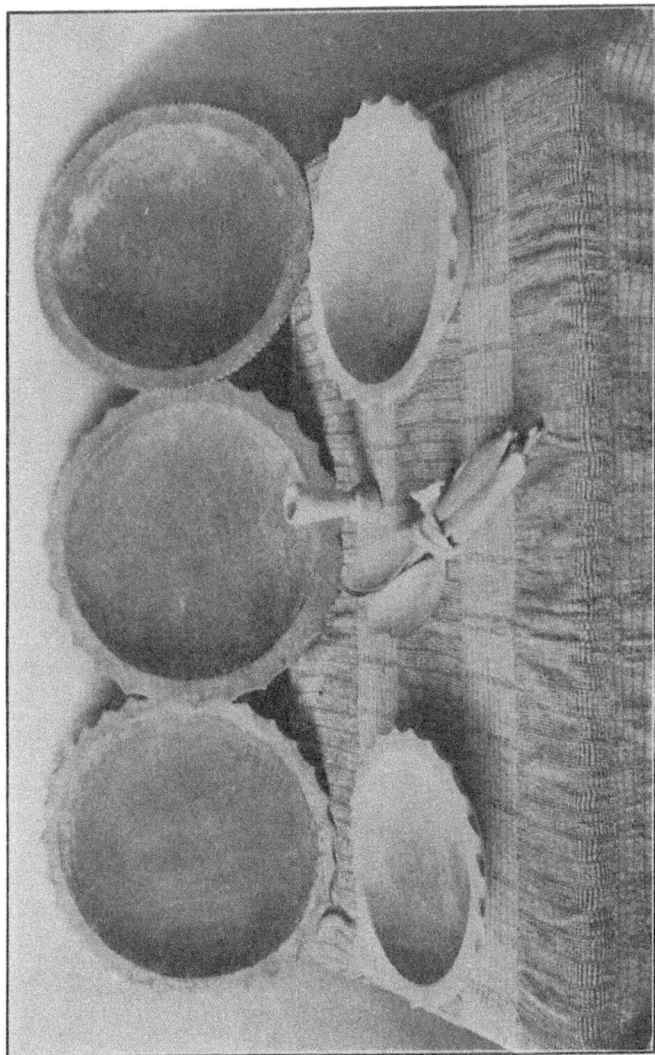

VAI WOODEN PLATES, SPOONS AND MORTAR

the money man to preach to-day for we. You can't say go call the king but the man who know book.

Affirmative. Money is fine pass book sense. If it's Sunday, the people get ready for to go church, go catch my big bullock for to kill him to-day for dinner, catch my sheep and kill him, and my goat. You can't say go bring book sense and kill him because it is God's day.

Judge N'fah Alihu. You all two tell the truth, but you all go for this man Momoru Lamene, because he be king for all judges.

Negative. Book sense is fine pass the money because that time you get ready for marry you can say go call the Mori man, and the man who know the book so he can come and see the play they live marry. They can't say go call the money man.

Affirmative. Money is fine, it pass book sense, if you no got money how can you marry? If you no got house, how can you marry? If you no got money, you can't marry. If you no got all these things, how can you marry? The king say:

Lamene. If a man no got book sense, and the same man no got money, the person die soon is better pass him live. All you all go find book sense any time because book sense is the thing that can cure person in this world. It can cure you in this world and when you die it can cure you again. You all find book sense and money.

So Momoru Lamene judged this matter for this two men. All people say: God give me book sense, you make we heart fine. Fix we heart how you like. The king fix we God. If you give to we book sense, you give to we money like you do the prophet Abraham.

TRANSLATION OF STORY NO. FIFTY-ONE

THE RASCAL MAN

One man live to take a walk to go for some place. He go and catch one big town. All the people join for play. They kill one cow. The man said, you all give to me cow head I buy him. Then all give it to him. He catch him and carry him far away. He go and catch big swamp. Some people live pass. He tell the people my cow swamp done catch him, he can't come out. You all come help me, so we can pull my cow out of the swamp. The people say all right. Then they catch the cow head and he done come out one time. Then he said you all done kill my cow. That's the thing you pay sixty dollars for him. The people give to him the sixty dollars.

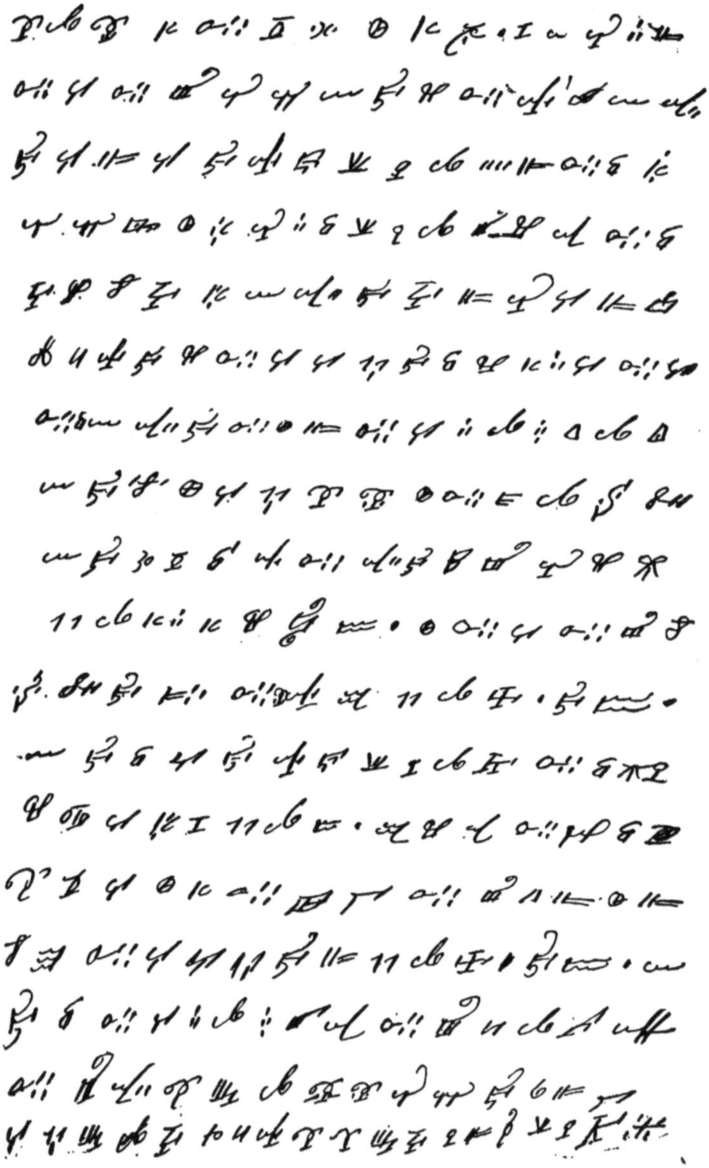

TRANSLATION OF STORY NO. FIFTY-TWO

THE SIX RIVAL HEIRS

One king born one daughter. Some person come for his daughter. No person can't marry this daughter. The person if he want to marry this girl, if I die, people must catch him and kill him for my burial. One fine young man come. He be some king's son. He come and say " Father, you all give to me your daughter." The man say, " If I die people can kill you for my burial." He said " all right." Then all give to him the girl. The boy carry the girl. He took her for his home. Soon he catch home, the king die. The people send messenger to him to call him. He went. The people say, " The king die. To-morrow we can kill you." He say, " All right." His wife in the night time took all her father's money and two horses.

At four A. M. in the morning she run away with her husband. Then day broke, the people go to the king's house. They no see all two. They send people to find him. They see them way yonder in an old field. The young wife is very thirsty. They two see one woman in an old field and say to her, " Give us some water. We give to you all the money we got and the two horses." The woman say, " No, if you all say I must give to you some water, if you are willing for me to become the wife of your husband, I can be willing." The young wife say, " All right." The old woman give all two some water. The people when they see the two in old field sat down. He sat down long time, then he got up and go and they say, " We want water." They see one

woman in old field. She live go to give chop to her working people. The people said, "Give to all we the chop
you live carry. We give to you the money we got."
The woman say, "No." She said, "I can't give to you
this chop. If you woman can agree for me to be wife
to your man, I can agree." The woman said, "Yes.
We can agree." She gave to them water. The working people die of hunger and for chop. They all go and
meet big river.

They go see one woman again, and this woman, her
people run away for war. This woman got canoe for
river. They tell the woman, "You cross we, we give
to you this money." The woman say, "I leave my
mother, then war catch him, for the money? If you
women agree that I have your man, then I can cross
we." The women say, "I agree." She crosses all the
people. When they all get in canoe and get out in the
river, the canoe stop, sit down. One woman live in
canoe got a baby. No person can cross this river for
nothing, before all can take good free born and put them
in the water, they die there. They tell the woman,
"Give to we your baby, so we can put he in the water,
give to you money." "For the money palaver I am
going to put my son in the water?" "If you don't do
that," the people say, "all we can die." The woman
say, "I agree." They put him baby in the water.

Then the canoe move. They cross the people. The
people all make six persons, five woman and one man.
This man carry all the money and all the women. One
woman say, "This money belong to all we, we must
divide it now." They divided it. They go to one king,
"We come to sit down to you." The king say, "All

right, but my things are here. My things, if any person call him name I can kill him." The people are scared. For true if you call him name the king kill you. The king said he had one girl his daughter. The daughter see this man and like him plenty.

The girl said, " I can't let you know this thing, him name." Night time the man go to bed, lay down. The king him daughter go lay down there. She tell him " To-morrow if my father bring anything, don't call him name." Soon in the morning the king bring all his things and say to the young man, " Call this thing his name." The young man say, " That is a picture for drinking and your whip." Soon as he called he name, the king died. This young man be king now. He got six wife now. Then all the women got born six boy. Then the man die. All the women die. The boys live. One boy say, " All the money belong to me." The other five boy say, " How all belong to you one? " The boy say, " Mother be first wife." The next little boy say, " All the money belong to me because if it had not been for my mother giving water to your mother she no born you." Now the next little boy say, " Money all belong to me because had my mother not given chop to the mothers of both of you you no be born." The next little boy say, " Had not my mother crossed the mothers of all you none of you be born for them war catch all you mothers." The next little boy say, " The money all belong to me. When the canoe sit down in the river my mother sacrificed her child so all you mother could cross. But for my mother all you mothers live to die in the river." The next little boy say, " No, the money all belong to me because when you all mothers come to my mother's house but for the advice of my mother all you mothers die before you all born." Question, to whom does the money really belong?

CHAPTER X

VAI LANGUAGE, CULTURE, AND CONCLUSION

I N the name of science, white savants long proclaimed that the Negro was not a member of the human family. But in the eagerness of anthropologists to show the Negro's descent from the gorilla, the chimpanzee, and the orang-outang, they not only proved that he was a man, but demonstrated that his brain capacity, a little less than that of the white man,[1] is four and five-tenths inches greater than that of the Australian, and more than twenty inches above the capacity of the anthropoid apes. Until the complete triumph of Evolution scholars contended that the language of the Negro, like the chatter of the monkeys, sustained no relation to the languages of the races. Along with the hypothesis of the common origin of man from an antecedent form came the theory of the common origin of languages. Through the great labors of Prof. Max Müller and others the confusion concerning the origin of languages was straightened out, and the science of languages was securely established among the sciences. Recent philological studies in Africa reveal the common relationship which the languages of the Negro bear to the languages of the world.

As pointed out in the introduction, the Vai language belongs to the Mánde family,[2] which is the most impor-

[1] About five and nine-tenths inches.
[2] Introduction, p. 1.

tant language of the six or eight languages of the pure Negro stock. Like some languages of the Bantu and Sudanese tongues, Vai is very rich and musical when spoken properly. Its liquid flow is little disturbed by the logical element. An accented syllable is usually followed by one or more unaccented ones. By the ejection of vowels, and the ejection and insertion of consonants, by the uniform proportion of vowel and consonantal elements, and by the agreeable modulation in the variety and succession of vowels, in euphony, cadence, and melody Vai is made to surpass Arabic, French, or Italian.

A careful examination of this language discloses the fact that the Vai Grammar contains

" the same rational principles, the same general laws, the same regularity and organism of structure, as the grammar of other languages." [3]

A number of Vai roots are identical with those found in the Semitic and Indo-European tongues. The interjections are the same as found not only in these languages, but in most other languages. Four of the Vai demonstrative roots may be recognized as the same, both in the Indo-European and Semitic languages. A comparison betrays that the pronouns are similar, and that two of the numerals admit of comparison.

A further comparison would show a general affinity with European, Asiatic, and other African languages, and the comparison might be extended to include the American tongues.[4] The Vais have adopted some English

[3] Grammar of the Vai Language, pp. 5 and 6, by the Rev. S. W. Koelle.
[4] Grammatik der Gronlandischen Sprache, by S. Kleinschmidt

and Portuguese words, a few French, German, and Spanish, together with some Arabic ones that are employed mostly by the Islamic Vais. The Rev. Koelle used thirty-four sounds, made by letters of the alphabet and their combination, to represent the orthography of the Vai language. Like most languages, Vai forms its plural by suffixes, but it has no inflection, no signs for cases. Etymologically, the personal and possessive pronouns are identical in Vai, while the adjectives are derivative and are formed from other parts of speech by the addition of suffixes.

The system of Vai numbers evidently grew out of the long custom of using the fingers and toes in counting. It is made up of quints, two for a decade and four for a score. Except the first five, the tenth, and the twentieth, all the cardinals are the result of combination. Of the ordinals only the first are in use. Verbs are generally followed by short adverbs of time, are usually formed by a suffix, and have no distinguishing sign for voice, mood, or tense. A vowel or combination of vowels make up the interjections. Substantives, adjectives, and verbs are interchangeable, just as pronouns, adverbs, and conjunctions are with one another.

In composition and decomposition substantives define or qualify adjectives, verbs, and substantives, but a verb can only qualify a substantive. Some words in compound undergo a change while others do not. The Vai language is highly figurative. Apposition, ellipsis, and pleonasm are common, comparisons are few, but fables, proverbs, and metaphors are abundant. The order of the chief elements of simple propositions is subject, then copula, then predicate. And in complex sentences, complements of subjects may be possessive pronouns, numerals, adjectives, and substantives in apposition. Pronouns, verbs, and substantives take many suffixes to give either the verbal or adverbial character. Vai has no case terminations, but the deficiency is made up by postpositions, interjections, and possessive pronouns. It consists generally of monosyllabic and dissyllabic words, and because of its national orthography is of peculiar interest to the linguistic world.[5]

THE HISTORY OF WRITTEN LANGUAGE

About ninety-six years ago in a quiet Vai town a Negro boy was born. He was afterwards given the name of Momoru Doalu Búkere,— Muhammud Bookman Gunwar. When quite a small boy for three months he was taught to read by a missionary in his country. This instruction, though brief, was sufficient to awaken in him a desire for learning, and he memorized some verses from the English Bible. By traders and slave-stealers he was afterwards employed as a servant. Often he carried notes to neighboring towns and brought back answers which contained information of some misdeeds he had done. This means of communication deeply impressed Doalu, and strengthened his aspiration to read and write. Indeed, the necessity for a mode of writing of their own had been generally felt by the proud Vai men, to make them equal as they thought to the Mandingoes and the Poros,— Europeans.

The ambition to read and write was so uppermost in the mind of Doalu that when he was about twenty-five years old he had a dream. In his vision he saw " a tall, venerable-looking white man, in a long coat," who said :

[5] I have made frequent use of the Rev. Koelle's Grammar in studying the Vai language. In many instances I have verified and found my conclusions in harmony with his valuable treatise.

"I am sent to bring this book to you by other white men. I am sent to bring this book to you, in order that you should take it to the rest of the people. But I must tell you that neither you nor anyone who will become acquainted with the book are allowed to eat the flesh of dogs and monkeys, nor of anything found dead whose throat was not cut; nor to touch the book on those days on which you have touched the fruit of the To-tree." [6]

The bearer of the book showed Doalu how to write any word in the Vai language, after the manner of the Vai writing, and promised to tell him the contents of the book. But Doalu awoke before he received the information. So powerfully was he influenced by the dream that the next morning he called his brother, Dshara Bara-kora, and his cousins,— Dshara Kali, Kalia Bara, Fa Gbasi, and So Tabaku,— and related to them his experience. They believed the dream was a divine revelation, and they were so much impressed that Kali Bara said he afterwards dreamed that the book was from God. By the next morning Doalu had forgotten some of the characters, and he and his five relatives were obliged to put their heads together and supply them. The result of their labors constitutes the first system of writing which is now known to have been invented by a Negro.

This system is a wonderful invention, original and independent. With upwards of 200 characters, it is unlike any of the written languages of the world. It is a syllabic mode of writing, and therefore different from Latin and Arabic and other alphabetical systems. It

[6] To-tree, a kind of very sharp pepper. "Narrative of an Expedition into the Vai Country of West Africa and the Discovery of a System of Syllabic Writing," by the Rev. S. W. Koelle.

corresponds in this respect with the syllabic nature of the spoken Vai. It is written from left to right, the reverse of Arabic, with the letters disjoined as in Hebrew. It has but a few symbolic characters, yet it is phonetic. While each character represents a syllable in monosyllabic words, it stands for the same sound in combinations. This system therefore is of Vai origin, and must be credited to the Negro brain.

This system of Vai writing was first discovered in January, 1849, by Lieutenant Forbes, who stopped at Fourah Bay to ascertain if the missionaries of Sierre Leone had ever heard whether or not there was a mode of writing among the native Africans. While at Cape Mount the Lieutenant had observed some indistinct characters written with charcoal on the walls of an old house. He examined these queer signs and announced the discovery of the Vai system of writing in a pamphlet entitled,

" Despatch communicating the discovery of a native-written character, etc., by Lieutenant F. E. Forbes, R. N."

In this pamphlet were some grammatical remarks by E. Norris, Esq., who has the honor of having been the first to study the Vai writing critically. He was followed by the Rev. S. W. Koelle, who came to Cape Mount in 1850, and who, after a residence of five months there, published his valuable " Grammar of the Vai Language."

The Rev. Koelle had the great privilege of meeting Momoru Doalu Búkere personally, and I have relied almost entirely upon the valuable information which he gives concerning Doalu and his invention. This great Negro inventor was distinguished by his modesty and nobility of spirit. In addition to being open, kind, and honest, he was a great thinker; and the product of his brain entitles him to a place among the great inventors of the world. I cannot resist the temptation to attach to this thesis as important parts of it, specimens of Vai writing and a Phonetic Chart of the Vai characters, by Momolu Massaquoi, Prince of Gallinas.

ELEMENTS OF VAI CULTURE

A few years ago the statement that the Negro had a culture in Africa would have been greeted with wonder and amazement by the great majority of the civilized peoples of the world. It seemed almost impossible for them to think of the Negro other than as a little above the savage beasts, roaming unrestrained amid the dark and tangled jungles. But these delusions are being rapidly dispelled. We have already partly seen how for centuries from Egypt, Nubia, Abyssinia, and the Barbary States the streams of Arabian culture emptied into the Negroland; pilgrimages were made in order to obtain the learning of Mecca and Medina, and the persons that made these pilgrimages secured from Cairo much of the Civilization of the East. When the Saracens were finally driven from Spain the Moorish scholars and poets carried to the Blacks the wealth and harvests of Grenada and Cardova.

Among the Negroes were established centers of learning, in which rhetoric, logic, eloquence, diction, and the principles of the Koran were given to the theologians. Law according to Malakite and artistic writing were taught to the jurists. There were regular courses of instruction in hygiene, medicine, grammar, prosody, philosophy, ethnography, music, and astronomy. A number of Negro authors became distinguished for their writings on traditions, biographies, annals, law, music, history, and theology. Negro scholars rivaled their Arabian masters. Their apartments, near the mosque of Sankore, were said to be to Timbuctu, the " Queen of the Sudan," what the " Quartier Latin '" is to Paris. Among the distinguished marabuts and eminent Negro writers M. Dubois mentions Mohaman Kati and Ahmed Baba; the former was the author of Fatassi, a history of the kingdoms of Ganata, Songhai, and the City of Timbuctu, and the latter wrote more than twenty books. In Baba's library there were fewer books than there were in the libraries of any of his friends, yet he had 1600 volumes. The learning and scholarship of the Sudanese Negroes was so thorough that,

" During their sojourns in the foreign universities of Fez, Tunis, and Cairo they astounded the most learned men of Islam by their erudition. That these Negroes were on a level with the Arabian savants is proved by the fact that they were installed as professors in Morocco and Egypt." [7]

It is therefore from the Arabs and the learned Negroes of the Sudan that the Vais received the Arabian culture. Belonging to the same family as the Mandingoes, the Vais easily accepted this culture. I do not mean to say that every Vai Muslim is deeply cultured any more than every Frenchman or German is highly cultured in the principles of Christian Civilization. The great masses of the greatest nations, with all the advantages of improved presses, good literature, and cheap books, have

[7] " Timbuctu the Mysterious," by M. Dubois, p. 285.

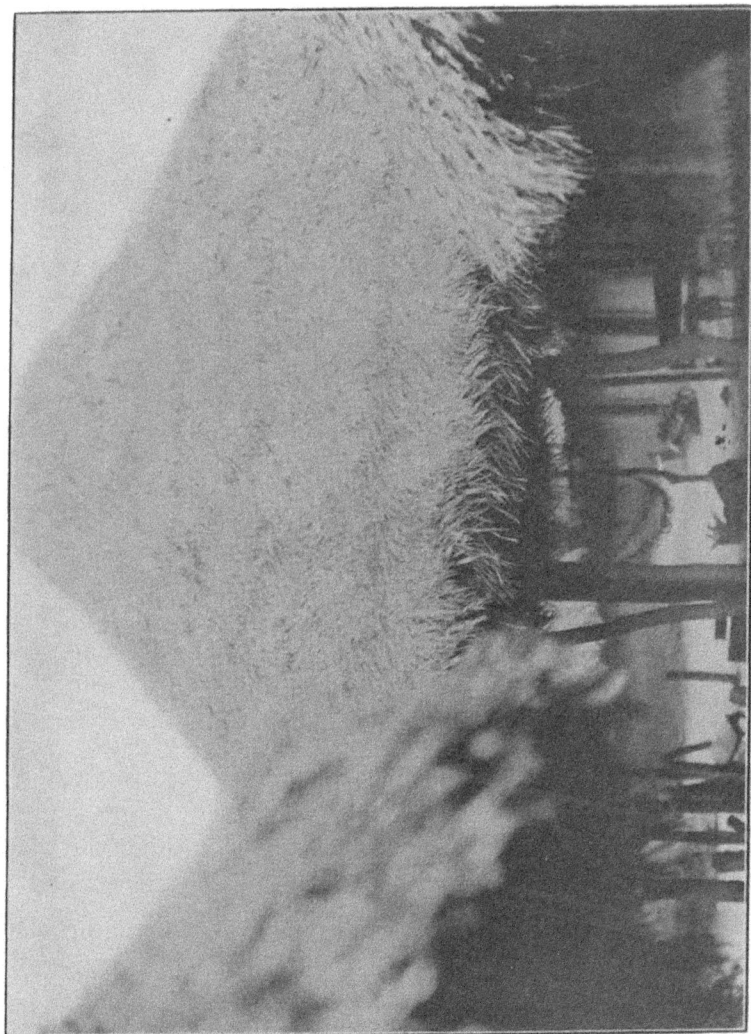

NATIVE VAI KITCHEN

not as yet risen above the mere struggle for bread. Among the Vais the majority of the books are written by hand. The lack of modern facilities for printing and making books not only makes them dear but scarce as well. Yet under all these difficulties, many of the Vais read and write Arabic; but with them as with other peoples culture and scholarship are reserved for the few who are willing to pay the price of their acquisition.

From what I have been able to learn I should judge that about 60% of the Vais are Muslims. For this they are chiefly indebted to the missionary labors of the Mandingoes, from whose ranks come, perhaps, the most eminent marabuts, schoolmasters, and scholars in Western Africa. The Mandingoes are widely and favorably known. Their industry, dignity, culture, and the breadth of their scholarship have made them so impressive that they are universally regarded by their neighbors as the "Gentlemen of West Africa." Culture is the result of knowledge. As it exists among the Vai scholars it has two fundamental phases: knowledge which the Vais acquired from experience and life under African conditions, and knowledge which has come to them from Arabia, through the Mandingoes, Mendis, and Arabs. From Arabian sources Vai Mallams,— like Murvey, Vahney, Seriff, Mambroru, Vahney Sonie, Boma Dadu, and Momoru Ducley,[8]— possess a varied fund of information that is as admirable as it is astonishing. They are familiar with geography and they talk of the countries and cities of the East as we speak of Europe. They are likewise acquainted with the general geography of the West. The better facilities for communication with

[8] See Library of Momoru Duclay, "Islamic Faith Among the Vais," pp. 128 and 129.

Europe and the founding of Liberia by Americans materially increased the geographic interest that was awakened by the slave traffic so many years ago among the Vais.

One is surprised at their knowledge of hygiene, physiology and the principles of medicine. Some of the cures which are effected by some of these Vai doctors simply stagger belief. Instances are cited where their surgeons have extracted bullets and set bones, removing fractured and shattered parts, that would have been a surgical triumph in any country. This seems incredible; but when you see a native doctor wash a man's hand in a medical solution, then see that hand thrust into boiling palm oil and withdrawn without pain or injury, something suggests to the strongest incredulity that perhaps these peoples have learned something yet unknown to modern science.

The Vai scholar and priest not only reads and writes Arabic fluently, but he knows the Koran by heart and can recall its varied parts without apparent difficulty. With numerous commentators, black and white, he discusses the tenets of this book in the light of the critical interpretation of the profoundest Islamic scholars. Many of these priests have copies of the New Testament in Arabic, and they know of the life of Jesus and the principles of the Christian faith. As Dr. Blyden pointed out, they object to Christianity on account of its disintegrating influences upon the family and the state, on account of caste distinctions based on race, and on account of the liquor traffic carried on by individuals living among Christian nations.[9]

[9] "Journal of the African Society," January, 1905, and "The Koran in Africa," by Dr. Blyden.

However, these objections should not be charged to Christianity. For while Christianity may tend to disintegrate the Negro family, founded upon polygamy, in the truest and best sense it is a great integrating and socializing factor among peoples who are prepared to understand and practice Christian principles, and who have not the weaknesses and the prejudices of undeveloped minds. Unquestionably the polygamic family is inconsistent with the highest social and spiritual development of mankind. So that the objection to Christianity on this ground might better be replaced by requiring that the destruction of polygamy in Africa be accompanied by the modern agents for progress and development that are suitable to the peculiarities of African environment.

So far as concerns the objection to Christianity on account of caste distinctions based on race, it cannot be argued that Christianity favors any such distinctions. In dealing with the Negro the white race has shown itself amazingly incompetent to think without prejudice or to act justly along progressive lines.[10] The white man has naturally confused difference with inferiority, to the great detriment of the Negro race. Christian Civilization has done a great deal to correct this error, but as yet it has not been able wholly to eradicate the evil. Some of the greatest friends the race has had have come from the ranks of the Christian Church, and some of the strongest influences working for the advancement of the race today are maintained and supported by the followers of the Cross. Unreasonable caste distinctions founded on race must vanish before the steady march of genuine

[10] The attitude of the white race in South Africa and the Southern States in America.

Christianity. So far as Christians and the Christian Church discriminate against the Negro it only discloses that the discriminators have not been able as yet, with all the advantages of modern life, to measure up to the high standard set by the peerless Prince of Peace. And waiving all other arguments, instead of objecting to the principles of Christianity on account of the practices of some Christians, would it not be wise for the Negro in Africa to accept those principles and furnish the world the example of what the true Christian ought to be?

As to the objection to Christianity because some persons in Christian countries engage in the liquor traffic, it is altogether unreasonable, for there are few things so generally opposed by Christians as the liquor habit. The opposition of the Christian Church to this habit is well known, but every person living among Christian nations is not a Christian. The demand for strong drink is so great that in every Christian nation there are individuals who are willing to brave the public scorn and suffer penalties in order to secure the profits of the liquor trade. Its prohibition may be possible, but that at least is something exceedingly difficult to accomplish. The liquor traffic is a curse to Africa, but it cannot properly be charged to Christianity. It is an evil of society just as slavery was in America. When Christianity and Civilization have wrought sufficient progress among the nations the liquor traffic will be stopped. For the African to reject Christianity for this reason shows that he does not know where to place the responsibility for the liquor trade.

I heard two very able Islamic scholars, Sareef and Mulahe, deny that Jesus was the Son of God miraculously conceived. They were willing to admit that he was a good man, but they denied His divinity. They proceeded

to condemn Christianity on account of what they called
the wonderful difference between the theory and the practice of Christians; and they dogmatically asserted the
consistency between the Koranic principles and Muslim
practices. The above objections and many others which
might be given, while untenable, nevertheless indicate the
character of the work to be done by the Christian Church
in bringing Islamic Negroes under the sway of the Cross.
The ablest Christian teachers are needed to secure the
best results.

From Arabian sources Vai scholars also secure valuable
information about statecraft and the art of war. The
influence of Arabian models may be seen in the cut of
their dress, and in the designs that they use in fashion-
ing useful and decorative arts. Works on music written
by Negro and Arabic scholars are common; and much
of the inspiration for the higher class of Negro music
may be traced easily to the East. Some of the Vai
scholars have a wealth of literature by Sudanese and
Arabic authors on a wide range of subjects, among which
might be named poetry, philosophy, theology, and
ethics.

But, after all, the native element in Vai culture is the
most interesting and important, for it is by the development of this element that the Vais have been able to em-
brace Islam and their scholars to absorb foreign culture.
The Vais have much knowledge and skill in the industrial
arts. From wood, iron, grass, gold, and silver they have
long known how to fashion products for useful and decorative purposes. They manufacture and dye cloth in
varied figures and designs. They possess considerable
knowledge regarding the utility of vines and the medicinal
qualities of roots and herbs. They have men familiar

with great systems of law founded on equity, and with the aim and philosophy of government. They understand the influence of institutions and their importance and value to society as methods to develop ethical culture. They have a written language, originated by a Vai man, with more than 200 characters. In their traditions, myths, legends, songs, and tales of romance they have an African literature.

Of the numerous Vai writings some may be seen by persons traveling through the Vai country in manuscript form and others on wooden tablets. Perhaps the oldest and most interesting of these Vai writings is the autobiography of Ndole Wono. So far as is known it is the masterpiece of Vai literature. It contains an account of Wono's wanderings in the interior, his romantic adventure with a princess, and concludes with a tragic description of his mother's death. Indeed, it is a thrilling story, and it justified the publication which was given to it more than fifty years ago, through the interest and labors of the Rev. S. W. Koelle, a distinguished linguist of London.

Vai scholars keep in touch with the great Mandingan and other scholars. They are familiar with the literature of the Blacks and the Arabs in Sudan. Young Vai scholars are sent to Musardu, Timbuctu, and other centers in search of the broadest and deepest African culture. If we consider that the Vais invented their own written language; that their scholars have mastered their native literature; that they have committed the Koran to memory; that they are familiar with the Holy Bible and with the phases of its higher criticism; that they have probed Arabian civilization to its core; that they are the authors of songs and stories of charm and interest; that they speak several native tongues, and that they possess a fund of information on a variety of subjects, we can hardly condemn the critic who describes this people as " The Romans of West Africa." Under the reign of peace this is a tribe of promise and power.

CONCLUSION AND NEGRO CIVILIZATION

From the preceding chapters on the Vai people I think we may safely draw the following conclusions:

First. The Vais, belonging to the Mánde branch of the Negro race, have been affected by the same forces that influenced the great Negroland from without, and according to the best known evidences they originated from the Mandingoes in the Hinterland of Liberia.

Second. In personal features the great majority of the Vais afford a flat contradiction to the generally accepted Negro type, although they live under climatic conditions characterized by the most severe and deteriorating influences.

Third. The economic life of the Vais, far from being dependent upon natural products, includes the cultivation of food materials, the sale of imported articles as well as of the products of their own industrial skill.

Fourth. The Vais live in social groups necessitated by physical conditions, and they maintain their various secret societies as means by which individuals are governed and prepared for native life. Witchcraft and the social dance are important factors in Vai life.

Fifth. The Government of the Vais is monarchial in spirit and form, divided into petty kingdoms, the authority of which to some extent is limited to the chief men of each kingdom and the traditional rights of free Vai men. With legislative, judicial, and executive functions, the Government has all the machinery for the detection and punishment of crime, the making and execution of laws, and the protection of life and property.

Sixth. The Vais have a conception of the true God, but their religious practice and worship are associated with fetiches, believed to be the abodes of indwelling spirits. A majority of the tribe believe in Islam, which has made concessions to Negro beliefs. Christianity has entered the field, and the Crescent may be succeeded by the Cross.

Seventh. The Vais have a high moral standard when they are under the sway of their own institutions, but they deteriorate under foreign influences, which destroy native restraints without supplying the elements of Modern Civilization. The medicine-man has both good influences and bad. The social institutions expose the people to grave moral dangers when they live near civilized centers and near the coast towns. But the Negro is not unmoral.

Eighth. In fundamentals the Vai language discloses its relationship to the great languages of the world, and it is rich and musical in the concord of its sounds. The written Vai language is a great invention of the Negro brain, original in conception and independent in character. The Vais have a culture of their own, divided naturally into two elements,— the native and the Islamic. Like other varieties of the Negro family, they have an African civilization which they have worked out for themselves, under the most degenerating and unfavorable circumstances. And when we shall have obtained a thorough knowledge of the conditions under which the Negro lives and are fully acquainted with his character, intellect, and life, we shall wonder, not that he has done so little, but that he has achieved so much.

By nature the Negro is an orator and diplomat. With

all his superstitions, his soul is rich in spiritual wealth. To his credit, he has an extinct civilization in Fezzan, which is older than the Carthaginians.[11] And long before the Arabs or Egyptians sent their culture across the desert Negro intellect had asserted itself in Sudan.

"From remotest antiquity Africans," says Reclus, "even beyond Egypt, took part in man's triumphs over nature. . . . The civilized world is indebted to the native for several domestic animals. . . . Even in industries Africa has contributed to the inheritance of mankind. The monuments of Egypt cannot all have been the work of the Rotu (Egyptians) alone. Among the products of Egyptian industry are frequently recognized forms recurring in Nubia and Sudan. Smelting and working iron have been attributed to the Negroes."

The Negroes of the Gold Coast manufactured gold wire chains so fine that they can scarcely be imitated abroad.[12] The steel chains of the Monbuttoo Negroes compare with similar productions of Europeans.[13] And Peschel says the Negroes in Bambara, Bambook, and Bornu not only make gunpowder but secure the saltpetre in their own country.[14] The Negroes build bridges that are greater than were those of the Germans in the time of Tacitus. And unaffected by foreign influences many Negro tribes have risen in Africa above the level of the Britons whom Cæsar saw. Some of them manufacture soap, and in portions of Sokoto they have courts paved

[11] "Redemption of Africa," by F. P. Noble, Vol. I, p. 168.
[12] "Guinese Goud Taud-en Slavekust," Vol. I, p. 123, by Bosman.
[13] "In the Heart of Africa," by Schweinfurth.
[14] "The Races of Man," by Oscar Peschel, p. 479.

with mosaic. Many products of the Mandingan art have occasioned the most favorable comment.

The Zambesi and Congo peoples originated empires and republics, which had complex governmental machinery. Unaided, Uyoro Negroes developed a government the administration of which included taxes and sub-governors, and their industry found expression in art, architecture, agriculture, and good clothes. In the great states of Dahomey and Ashantee Negro civilization attained considerable heights. It is said the high quality of Dahoman culture drew words of commendation from so able an authority as Herbert Spencer. And when the Moors sought to penetrate Nigretia there rose up a Negro, by the name of Soni Heli Ischia, who beat them back and established across Africa an empire three thousand miles in length,— extending on one side from Timbuctu to Abyssinia, and on the other to the sea.[15]

In this great Negroland powerful states and dynasties rose and fell. Their universities sent out Negro professors whose scholarship astonished the most learned men in the intellectual centers of Morocco, Tunis, and Egypt. So that as little as we know of Africa and the Africans, in comparison to the great deal that is unknown, it is quite evident that in material progress, self-government, and statecraft the Negro has made advancement in a region where — as yet, to any appreciable extent,— the white man has not been able to remain and live.

[15] "Christianity, Islam, and the Negro Race," Dr. Blyden, p. 141.

Northwestern Africa

The Geographical Publishing Co.
Chicago, Ill.

INDEX

INDEX

division of power, 75; crime and justice in, 82, 84; Vai forms of, 273.
Polygamy, 58, 269; See family; tolerance of Islam, 126.
Pomopora, 78; oath of, 79.
Population, the Vais, location and study of, 11; Liberian, Vais as, 12.
Populations, great desert and Congo basin, 11; native, 13.
Poros, European, 262; See European.
Portuguese, words in, 262.
Priests, dress of, 38, 94; See Vais; Islamic, 110, 268.
Prince of Peace, 270.
Problems, native tribes as, 13; contribution to, 15.
Prosody, Negro instruction in, 265.
Protestant Episcopal Church, 111.
Proverbs, 18; Elephant and Bridge, Monkey and Honey, Skillet and Soup, 147; Baboon and Cola, Pig and Liquor, Catfish and Straw, Man and Leopard, 148; Man and Snake, Cow and Salt, Man and Beans, 149; Little Rain, Frog and his Hop, Man and Monkey, Stomach and Palaver, 150; Go in or by, Greegree Bush and Cloth, 151; Hens and Milk, Gourd and Bowl, Naked Man and Soap, 152; Dog and Blacksmith Shop, Man and Empty Plate, Lazy Man behind, 153; Spear and Banana Tree, Crazy Man and Slaves, 154; Poor Children for Rich, Featherless Chicken, Country Devil, 155; Person looking with his Foot, Chicken with red Leg, Absent Man and Funeral, 156; Paddle and Canoe, Leopard and Cat, 157; Bad Goat, Wise Man and Fool, Small Bird and Boil, 158; Lame Man and Carrier, Mushroom and Bugabug Hill, Small and large Palm Nuts, 159; Owner and Cook, Rich Hired Man and Owner, 160; Rice-cutter and Rice, Running Snake and its Head, Swimming Man Feet, 161; Food in Mouth First, Moon and Dark Places, Two old Ladies, Dry Leaf on Tree, Hand in a Hole, 163; Boy and Cola Tree, Boy up a Tree, 164; Bird and Hole in Pot, War and Play, Goat and the Mud, 165; Leopard and Skin, Shame Man and Crawfish, 166; Bugabug Hill and Mushroom, Frizzle Chicken and Town Doctor's Work, 167; Old Hen and Town, Billy Goat and Jewelry, 168; Knowledge and the Goat's Head, Grippa and Fish, Dogmeat Cold, 169; String and Grass, Trouble and Your Pocket, 170; Cassava

and Stomach, Old Lady and Market, Satisfied Stomach, 171; One Man and Two Places, Cow and Horse, 172; Running and Cracked Foot, Man and New Moon, Man and his Way, 173; The Pretty House, Old Cloth, Playing Organ at Night, Sassy Woman, Horn and Gun, 174; The Piles, Man and His Well, Rice Bird and Little Billy Goat, Bamboo Stick and Reed, 175; The Pestle and Flour, Chicken and Teeth, Man and Monkey, Elephant and Tusks, Man and Head Cut off, 176; Catching Cat by Neck, Rain and the Orange, Water and the Fish, Flour in Two Hands, 177; Fish and Water, Goat in Cowtown, Liar and Sleep, Water and Skin, 178; Meat and Goat, Leopard and Chicken, The Man with Enough Food, Little Birds Crying, 179; Elephant and Head, Doctor and Baby, Licking Hand, Snake at the Well, 180; At Bottom of Sea, Bag and Leopard Hide, The Minnow and his Deep, Dried Rat, To Strike with Rock, 181; Water Pot and Drinking, Man and Singing, Eating Raw Cassava, Carried by Messenger, 182; Walking with Nothing, 183.
Psychology, 18.
Pushkin, Alexander, poet, 19.

Q

Queen Anne, touched by, 61.
Quartier, Latin, 266.

R

Race, matters of, 14, 21; human race, 33; immorality of, 128; See Negro.
Races, truth to be given to, 19; cooperation of, 20; love in, 56; inferiority of black, 102.
Ramadhan, 97.
Reclus, Elisee, 98, 99; estimate of, 100; quoted on Negro, 275.
Reade, Winwood, 31, 32; of West Africa, 275.
Red Sea, mouth of, 22, 95, 101.
Reformation, 61.
Religion, 85, 122, 123.
Religious, writers, 14, 85, 86, 96, 125; ceremonies, 87, 88; gifts of, 87; the palm tree in, 88; sacrifices, 86, 87, 88, 89, 90, 92, 94; function of medicine-man, 92; alligators in, 88; natural phenomena in, 91; violation of laws, 93; faith and practice, 95, 123; conceptions, 105; Vai practice and forms, 274.

www.ingramcontent.com/pod-product-compliance
Lightning Source LLC
Chambersburg PA
CBHW040144270326
41929CB00024B/3363